Gentleman
Spies

SEMPER MIRABILIS

M.I.R.

Gentleman Spies

INTELLIGENCE AGENTS IN
THE BRITISH EMPIRE
AND BEYOND

JOHN FISHER

SUTTON PUBLISHING

First published in 2002 by
Sutton Publishing Limited · Phoenix Mill
Thrupp · Stroud · Gloucestershire · GL5 2BU

British Library Cataloguing in Publication Data
A catalogue record for this book is available from the British Library.

ISBN 0-7509-2698-8

Typeset in 11/14.5pt Sabon.
Typesetting and origination by
Sutton Publishing Limited.
Printed and bound in England by
J.H. Haynes & Co. Ltd, Sparkford.

Contents

List of Plates

Half-title page: the drawing is from a homemade Christmas card sent to Teague-Jones/Sinclair by his colleagues in 1919. The legend on the back reads: 'Card from my pals in M.I.R. (Military Intelligence Russia) on the eve of my departure on another solo mission, this time with destination ? Hush. Hush!'

The cartoon of 1912 by W.K. Haselden which appears on page 130 is reproduced by kind permission of the *Daily Mirror* (Centre for the Study of Cartoons and Caricature, University of Kent, Canterbury).

The following cartoons used at chapter endings are from *My Adventures as a Spy* by Robert Baden-Powell (A.C. Pearson, 1915)

List of Plates

Note: Every effort has been made to trace the owners of copyright in the pictures included. If contacted, the author will be pleased to correct any errors and omissions in subsequent editions of this book.

Acknowledgements

Special thanks to:
Dr Andrew Tatham and staff at the Royal Geographical Society;
Trustees of the Imperial War Museum; staff at the Oriental and
India Office Collections of the British Library; Mr C. Gandy;
Churchill Archives Centre, Cambridge; Guildhall Library;
Mrs Bridget Grant; Foreign and Commonwealth Office;
Admiralty Library; Ministry of Defence; Surrey Record Office;
Mr Hugh Alexander; Hon. Artillery Company; Intelligence Corps
Museum; Liddell Hart Centre for Military Archives; Royal
Society for Asian Affairs; Library of School of Oriental and
African Studies; Nuffield College, Oxford; Mr Michael
Blackwood; National Library of Scotland; Leeds Russian Archive
and Mr C. Sheppard, Special Collections, Brotherton Library,
Leeds; The Travellers' Club; Western Manuscripts Section of the
Bodleian Library; Middle East Centre, St Antony's College,
Oxford; Centre for Kentish Studies; Manuscript Collections of
the British Library; Rhodes House Library; Mr Anthony Camp;
Glenalmond School; Archivists at the Universities of Aberdeen
and Manchester; Katy Green and BP Amoco Archive; Companies
House, Cardiff; Lloyds TSB; East Sussex County Council; Sir
John Soane's Museum; Royal Institute of International Affairs;
Abingdon School; Trinity College, Cambridge; National Library
of Ireland; Royal Archives, Windsor; RAF Benevolent Fund; RAF
Association; Museum of the Argyll and Sutherland Highlanders;
News International; Samfundet for Dansk, Genealogiog
Personalhistoric; Mr David List; Northamptonshire County

Acknowledgements

Record Office; Old Wellingtonian Society; Rafatrad Ltd; Public Record Office of Northern Ireland; Metropolitan Police Museum; Mrs A. Whittall; Phil Tomaselli; Air Historical Branch; East Sussex County Council.

* * *

Readers who have delved into the archives to research intelligence history will, I hope, understand the extensive archival searches necessary for this book. Unlike some authors I have not benefited unduly from the cooperation of the Secret Intelligence Service. Consequently, my debt to those institutions and individuals who have courteously responded to many obscure enquiries, or who have afforded me access to papers in their care, is immense. I am also most grateful to Christopher Feeney, Paul Ingrams and Sarah Flight of Sutton Publishing for their enthusiasm and interest in this book and for their professional yet friendly approach. I am indebted to Professor Jeremy Black for his support and interest in this project and for publishing in *Archives*, in an earlier form, versions of two chapters of this book. I am similarly indebted to many colleagues at the Public Record Office who have often helped my research by answering questions in areas that I know little about. For their interest in this book, I am grateful to Professor Michael Dockrill, Oliver Hoare, Dr Thomas Otte, Professor Keith Neilson, Dr Keith Wilson and Professor Erik Goldstein, to Trudy and Peter Francis and to my family. I am most grateful to Michelle for her support and kindness. This book is dedicated to my mother who, many years ago, in the depths of a Highland winter, first handed me a copy of John Buchan's thriller, *The Thirty-Nine Steps*.

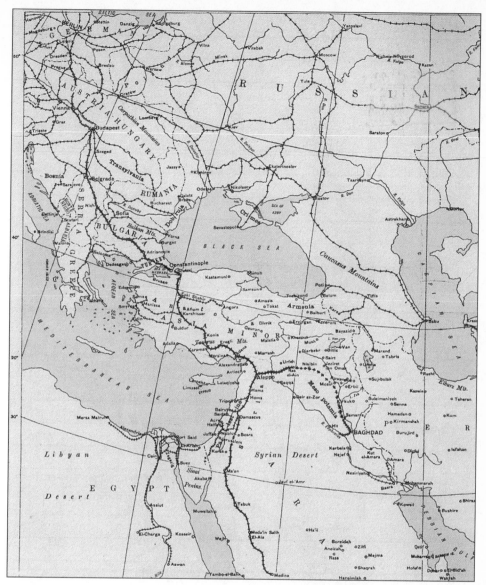

1 General map of the Middle East, Central Asia and Arabia, showing the line of the Baghdad railway. (*PRO. By permission of the Controller of Her Majesty's Stationery Office*)

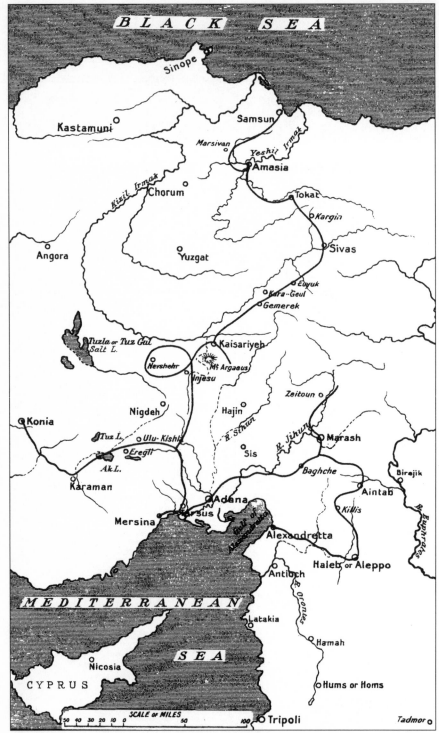

2 Childs's travels between Samsun and Alexandretta, from *Across Asia Minor on Foot*. (*Blackwood, 1917*)

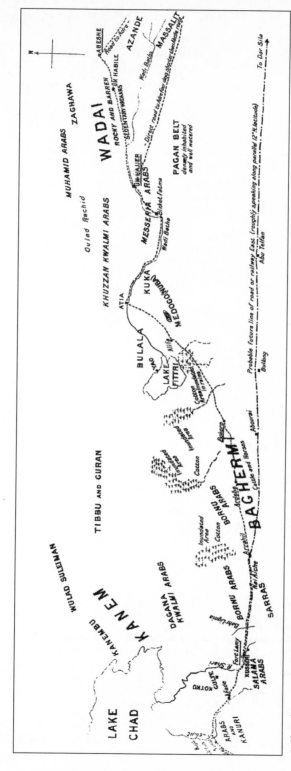

3 Sketch map to illustrate report on journey through Territoire du Chad by H.R. Palmer, May 1919.

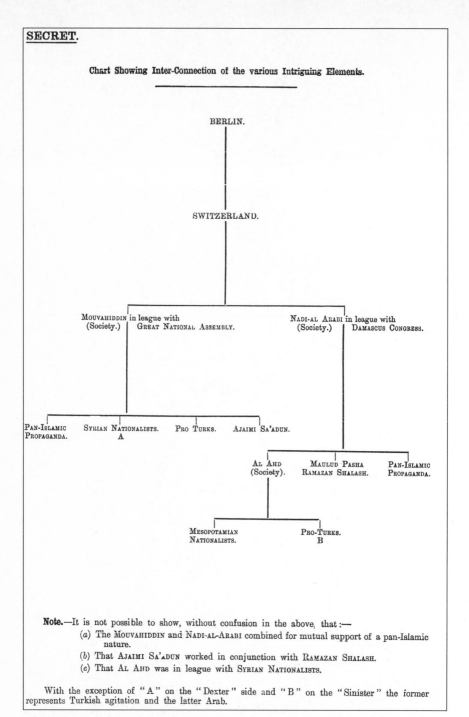

Chart Showing Inter-Connection of the various Intriguing Elements.

BERLIN.

SWITZERLAND.

MOUVAHIDDIN in league with   NADI-AL ARABI in league with
(Society.)   GREAT NATIONAL ASSEMBLY.   (Society.)   DAMASCUS CONGRESS.

PAN-ISLAMIC   SYRIAN NATIONALISTS.   PRO TURKS.   AJAIMI SA'ADUN.
PROPAGANDA.   A

AL AHD   MAULUD PASHA   PAN-ISLAMIC
(Society).   RAMAZAN SHALASH.   PROPAGANDA.

MESOPOTAMIAN   PRO-TURKS.
NATIONALISTS.   B

Note.—It is not possible to show, without confusion in the above, that :—

(a) The MOUVAHIDDIN and NADI-AL-ARABI combined for mutual support of a pan-Islamic nature.

(b) That AJAIMI SA'ADUN worked in conjunction with RAMAZAN SHALASH.

(c) That AL AHD was in league with SYRIAN NATIONALISTS.

With the exception of " A " on the " Dexter " side and " B " on the " Sinister " the former represents Turkish agitation and the latter Arab.

4 'Secret' Foreign Office chart showing how the various 'intriguing elements' of Islamic extremism fitted together internationally. Similar charts probably adorn the walls of the Pentagon today. (*PRO. By permission of the Controller of Her Majesty's Stationery Office*)

Briefings

In the higher ranges of Secret Service work the actual facts in many cases were in every respect equal to the most fantastic inventions of romantic melodrama. Tangle with tangle, plot and counter-plot, ruse and treachery, cross and double-cross, true agent, false agent, double agent, gold and steel, the bomb, the dagger and the firing party were interwoven in many a texture so intricate as to be incredible and yet true. The Chief and the high officers of the Secret Service revelled in these subterranean labyrinths, and amid the crash of war pursued their task with cold and silent passion.

Winston Churchill, *Thoughts and Adventures* (London, 1947)

Into the Labyrinth

One evening in the winter of 1987/8 a history undergraduate at the University of Glasgow sat reading in his room in the city's West End. The high tenement building in which he lived was built on a slope, so that, had anyone been so inclined, entering into a gated garden at its rear, they might have observed clearly the windows of the ground-floor rooms of the house, including that of the student. From the pages of a Dickens or Hardy novel – such was his taste in reading – the student was suddenly distracted by the noise of footsteps, slow but confident and, at a guess, made by good, hard-soled shoes, approaching his window in the darkness on the gravelled path. He had the impression, somehow, that the observer, whilst wishing to remain unseen, did not care to adopt the measured stealth of a burglar. The visitor did not stay long. Whatever he sought (I suspect it was indeed a man), he seemed to confirm with little delay. Precisely the same events reoccurred in the following year, by which time the student, and his shadow, had moved to new lodgings.

My contact, my brief official contact, with the Secret Intelligence Service (SIS), began in the summer of 1990 shortly after graduation. Quite why that organisation or its 'talent scouts' considered me fit for a career in intrigue and excitement I am apparently never to know; that information being so sensitive as to imperil national security should it be divulged – or so I am told. One possibility, besides the more obvious one of having been recommended by a university tutor, is a brief association I had with an Iraqi biochemist, whom I will simply refer to as

'Dr M.'. In 1987, he was involved in post-doctoral work on the use of chemicals in agriculture and, as we shared lodgings throughout that year, I came to know him and to appreciate his intelligence, his fervent devotion to the Muslim faith, and his affable nature. His political bearings and views about the world situation and international relations remained a mystery. On one occasion, I accompanied Dr M. to an industrial fair at the Scottish Exhibition Centre in Glasgow. He attended as a research fellow in biochemistry interested in commercial developments in his field and I – I now confess – appeared in the guise of a British Petroleum official, who had failed earlier to attend and claim his name badge. What Dr M. almost certainly did not mention to the exhibitors or, for that matter, to anyone but me, was that he held the rank of Major in Saddam Hussein's Army; something that he demonstrated by means of a photograph, having first sworn me to secrecy.

The letter, when it arrived in a luxurious manila envelope, asked me to attend a short 'exploratory discussion' at an address just east of the Admiralty Arch in London's Whitehall. From that moment on, I became mesmerised by the obvious career possibilities at which the letter hinted. My interviewer, a 'Mr Michael Halliday' – or one who employed that alias – apparently had also interviewed the 'renegade spy' Richard Tomlinson. He was, as I recall, rather taller than Tomlinson has suggested. He had a distinguished appearance and was without sign of the string vest that singled him out in Tomlinson's mind. He did, as I recall, wear heavy, steel-toecapped shoes; something that, to my youthful and impressionable mind, seemed to enforce his claim that members of his organisation, whilst they did not seek out confrontation, would know how to handle themselves in a tight corner. On his desk, I recall a photograph of a young man in the uniform of a Metropolitan Police Officer – a son or nephew, perhaps; the former, I now suspect, in view of his comments about the need for absolute discretion, even with close family members. He also, rather surprisingly, let slip the identity of another student from my university who had been invited to interview that summer by SIS. There ended my first encounter with that most secretive of government bodies.

Like any other young man I was gripped, and still am, by the thrill of espionage, its history and its portrayal in other mediums. The 'recruitment interview' is a moment that has been captured by writers and filmmakers. Indeed, my emotions and actions immediately afterwards are echoed in the recollections of another, rather more successful Secret Service recruit, Paul (later Sir Paul) Dukes, whose story from revolutionary Russia during the First World War is told in Chapter 6. Writing in his book, *The Story of 'ST 25'*, Dukes recalled:

> I went out and sat down in St James's Park. With whirling emotions I reflected on the invitation that had been made to me. . . . But the Secret Service was to me an utterly unknown quantity, and in so far as I could imagine it at all, I could not conceive that I had any aptitude for it whatsoever . . . I would play my part to the utmost of my ability. And just as, over there in Flanders, hundreds of thousands of my countrymen were prepared, in violation of every humane instinct, but for service, systematically to delude, capture, kill, so I also, for service, must be prepared systematically to play a part, and obtain that information regarding the adversary which my leaders would require.

Dukes's departure from Russia in the late summer of 1919 was preceded by anxious efforts on the part of SIS to ensure his escape. The man picked for the task was a Royal Naval Officer, Lt Agar. Like Dukes, Agar recalled his first encounter with the head of SIS, Sir Mansfield Cumming:

> A feeling of pride and gratitude filled me as I looked straight into the eyes of this man, my Chief and my friend, who had suggested me for so unique a task. The next forty-eight hours appeared like one of those strange and vivid dreams where every detail stands out with startling and unforgettable clearness. It seemed to me as

if I was living in a George Henty short story specially written for the Boy's Own Paper of my childhood days in the nineties, but in which I was to play a part.

The methods and technologies of British intelligence gathering have advanced considerably since the First World War, but for many its intoxicating effect remains unchanged. Such was the effect upon a fictional character created by Reginald Teague-Jones, aka Ronald Sinclair, whose story is told in Chapter 1. In later life, besides publishing details of his own intelligence work, Jones or Sinclair turned his hand to writing a novel. Its protagonist, a young American officer, Captain Jim Allenby, is interviewed for a secret mission to investigate the intrigues of the 'Nawab of Mongrote' and of German emissaries beyond the Indian frontier. To Jim it was 'the very sort of thing I've always dreamed of'. Sinclair wrote: 'The gleam in Jim's eye and the ring in his voice were sufficient for the General. The boy was keen as mustard, he told himself, just as he had expected.'

Similarly, John Beverly Nichols, when asked in 1921 to report on the situation in Greece, recalled:

Would I go to Athens? Would I go to heaven? Just imagine if you had just come down from Oxford, were still at heart an undergraduate, and were suddenly given the opportunity of embarking on an adventure which gave every promise of situations as fantastic as ever occurred to the peppery imagination of William le Queux! For, naturally, one guessed that, in an undertaking of this sort, there would be a certain amount of danger. The Balkan countries have never been exactly a health resort for political adventurers, and what should I be but a political adventurer, delving into secrets about which, at the moment, I knew nothing, in a distant and romantic capital which was alive with intrigue?

Admittedly, Nichols went to Greece at the request of his publisher and not of SIS but he was well aware of the thin divide between travellers of any sort that then existed in the minds of those Whitehall mandarins who required up-to-date information. The thrill of the chase has not dimmed over the decades. Nowadays, though diplomats and journalists insist that the Great Game is over, clearly it is not and never will be as long as foreign policy remains the prerogative of the nation state. In fact, with its striking resemblance to worldwide unrest in the period immediately after the First World War, current international events point to a renaissance of espionage as an essential accompaniment to more warlike activities.

Deep Cover:
Problems of Researching the History of British Espionage

This book attempts to illuminate the nature of British intelligence gathering overseas in the first decades of the twentieth century. It is the result, not of privileged access to the archives of any intelligence agency, but of detailed research among many archives and libraries. It is not intended as an academic study but I will gladly supply document references to readers who wish to pursue their own research. Given these limitations and further restrictions of time and space, I hope that readers will find in each chapter insights into individual characters and the nature of Britain's broader overseas intelligence gathering as it emerged many decades ago.

Intelligence history is fraught with problems in terms of primary research. A determined researcher will, for example, find tantalising snippets of information about individual Secret Intelligence Service (SIS) officers and, with some perseverance, he or she may identify that officer by name or perhaps identify another who worked for other bodies with an interest in intelligence gathering and analysis. However, it is unusual to find collections of private papers left by such individuals, certainly by SIS officers. Where these exist, they tend not to dwell on secret matters. Clearly, there are some exceptions. In the earlier part of the twentieth century, there are the papers of Samuel (later

Sir Samuel) Hoare, who preceded Paul Dukes as head of the British Intelligence Mission in Russia. Likewise, after many decades of self-imposed silence and anonymity, Reginald Teague-Jones, or Ronald Sinclair, also left papers. Slightly later in the century, among other collections, there are those of H. Montgomery Hyde, who joined SIS in 1939. Similarly, whilst researchers have benefited from government initiatives to make 'sensitive' material publicly available, the material released from the archives of the secret services generally tells only part of the story. That is certainly so of Security Service (MI5) material released to the Public Record Office (PRO). The archive of SIS is officially closed, although a small collection of pre-1909 material has been made available. Of course, material generated by that body may, with determined research, be found among the papers of other government departments. Private papers, which may also be censored by central government prior to release, newspapers and other sources, can yield some material but the picture that emerges is seldom satisfactory.

Researchers have also to contend with the heavy hand of the weeder and of the scrutineer and with contemporary attitudes to secret intelligence. The payrolls of the pre-1909 foreign intelligence gathering service at the PRO list individuals by codename, not all of which can now be easily deciphered. During the First World War there was an understandable reluctance among senior military intelligence officers to have the names of officers of the Intelligence Corps appear in the printed *Army List*. Having exhausted the official sources, the researcher must also contend with loyalties to family members, long deceased, whose otherwise ordinary lives were interrupted by a period of intelligence gathering. Much time can be wasted by establishing probate details as a means of locating surviving family, only to be told that no material survives or, worse, to hear nothing at all in response to pleas for information.

The fact that many intelligence gatherers were also in uniform might encourage hopes of finding further details of their lives in surviving service records now at the PRO. However, in general, these contain only the sparest details of their secret employment. This was not apparently owing to a deliberate policy of retention or destruction by over-zealous scrutineers, but, in the case of Army service records at any rate, resulted from the weeding of 'non-essential' material where pensions and other financial obligations might exist. These records, whilst confirming involvement with a section of military intelligence, or indeed naval intelligence, often do little more than this. In exceptional cases they might provide additional insights into the career of an officer whose life suddenly took an 'exciting' turn.

Information about some of these individuals, whether of the armed forces or not and whether in uniform or not, can be gleaned from the service lists and the *War Office List*. We also know something of the structure and evolution of intelligence gathering overseas from detailed scrutiny of, among other departmental records, those of the Foreign Office, Treasury and War Office. Among the latter, now at the PRO, are those of M.R.K. Burge, who, when not writing poetry, worked for a branch of MI6, and left a series of memoranda on the emergence of British intelligence operations in various European countries.

Where, in some cases, intelligence duties broadened to encompass propaganda activities, the researcher might hope to find further information. In the case of one Hugh Whittall, who was later identified as a secret service officer, we know from Ministry of Information files at the PRO that, during the First World War, he was sent to Switzerland ostensibly with propaganda functions. Similarly, Ernest Shackleton was employed to undertake propaganda duties in South America, although few of his biographers appear to have recognised this, and information about this episode, though not about any other intelligence activities undertaken by him, can be found at the PRO. In later life Paul Dukes, whose career in espionage is described in Chapter 6, was also employed in the field of propaganda work and it is possible that there was not in the early part of the last century the sharp institutional division between the activities of intelligence gathering and analysis and propaganda that has since come to exist.

A Structure Emerges

I do not propose to reiterate at great length the structural development of British intelligence – military or political – as accounts of this now abound. Suffice it to say that, by the early years of the twentieth century, Britain's intelligence community was already diverse. In the British Isles and the empire, all manner of individuals were employed on intelligence duties by the War Office, by the Admiralty and by other government departments and this was reflected in the existence at the War Office of a special section of military intelligence devoted to the correlation of intelligence submitted by travellers and civilians of all kinds.

The Metropolitan Police had also been involved in secret work for several decades. In 1842, a plain-clothes branch was established at Scotland Yard and, despite persisting notions of ungentlemanly conduct associated with such work, a criminal investigation department (CID) followed in 1878 and a Special Branch in 1887. The activities of these bodies in their fight with political violence have been dealt with by other authors. Among the more notable members of those bodies were Robert Anderson and Thomas Beach (*alias* Henri le Caron). By 1909, and the formation of the Secret Service Bureau, there was, as Bernard Porter has written, a growing realisation that if Britain hoped to obtain certain kinds of information, she would have to employ the methods used by her adversaries, however unscrupulous. Of those detailed to combat the growing threats posed by Fenians and anarchists, William Melville, an Irishman and distinguished hurley player, stands out. Melville served with the Metropolitan Police for over thirty-one years, rising to the rank of Superintendent of CID. After considerable success in this rôle and many daring exploits, he became Vernon Kell's first detective in the domestic arm of the Secret Service Bureau. Melville was an accomplished linguist, a man of great personal courage and the recipient of many foreign awards. As Kell's detective in the early years of the twentieth century, he tackled, among other things, the alleged infiltration of the Legion of Frontiersmen by German agents, and undertook widespread intelligence-gathering operations against German suspects in Britain.

Less thrilling, perhaps, but no less important in terms of present-day espionage, there was the Commercial Intelligence Department of the Board of Trade. That body, founded in 1899, analysed information collected, among others, by travellers, British consuls and others who were specifically charged with the task of assembling knowledge of this kind. The intelligence-gathering activities of those individuals and of the Board of Trade later in the century have gone largely unnoticed by researchers.

With the emerging rivalry between Britain and Germany, the official response – from the Committee of Imperial Defence – was the creation of the Secret Service Bureau. Besides other measures, it was deemed wise to regularise intelligence on the continent and in Germany especially. The task fell to Lt Col, later Sir, James Edmonds, head of MO5, the section that preceded the Secret Service Bureau. Within two years the War Office and Admiralty jointly ran several agents in Germany – but Edmonds encountered a number of difficulties, not the least of which was the abiding opposition at the Foreign Office and elsewhere, to the notion of British officials and officers undertaking work that might have the appearance of being *underhand*. . . . The position improved slightly from 1912 with the appointment of Richard Tinsley as the leading agent at the centre of British operations in Germany and Holland.

The Secret Service Bureau in turn spawned the domestic and imperial intelligence service that came to be known as MI5,* and the foreign intelligence service under MI1c or MI6.** The

---

*   Now the Security Service.
** Also known as the Secret Intelligence Service.

energies of this foreign intelligence arm of the Secret Service Bureau were directed to countering threats from forces without the empire. However, it also took a keen interest in the interaction and destabilising effect of those threats from unstable or disloyal elements within it.

Some authors have drawn a sharp distinction between military and political intelligence and between those involved in espionage and those who analysed the material gathered by these operational agents, but I do not intend to do so in this book. For my investigations have suggested that very often the spy would also undertake analysis and the deskbound officer might also have periods of active information gathering. Whilst the gathering and transmission of information frequently exposed agents to great personal danger, it must be remembered that often their information consisted of dry and lengthy notes on political, economic and military subjects, which I have tried to bring to life. Very often, these notes constitute the bulk of the evidence for the very existence of their authors as intelligence personnel.

Of 'Adventure, Fun, Peril and Love'

Britain's intelligence community at the start of the twentieth century was structurally broad even in those early days; yet, its members were a relatively closely knit social group, tied by class, education and, in some cases, regimental or service affiliations. There were also cases of whole families being drawn into secret intelligence work. Prominent among these was the Whittall family – in fact, it was more of a dynasty – of Smyrna in Turkey. For nearly two centuries the Whittalls had major interests in the mohair trade in Asia Minor and they lived across the region. The writer Wilfred Macartney, who was himself on Secret Service duties in the eastern Mediterranean during the First World War, described them as a 'strongly marked race; shrewd; jolly fellows as keen in business as the Greek and Armenian combined'. He continued: 'They have also the vigour and bravery of the Turk.

A curious family, they are all Harrovians, and speak Turkish, Greek, French, Italian as well as, and sometimes even better than, English.' Hugh Whittall and his cousin Arthur Whittall were, like Macartney, both members of Compton Mackenzie's secret intelligence organisation; and, when Kim Philby was posted to Turkey in 1947, as First Secretary at the British Embassy, there was an officer apparently of the same Whittall clan serving with SIS in Constantinople.

Though it is widely assumed that intelligence officers in the early part of the last century took their secrecy seriously, this was not invariably the case. Several intelligence officers, Compton Mackenzie included, published memoirs in which details were given of intelligence personnel and of operations. In Mackenzie's case, this led, unjustly in some ways, to a court case at the Old Bailey and not, as had once apparently been mooted, the directorship of SIS. At his trial, Mackenzie was charged under the Official Secrets Act with having divulged sensitive information. Wilfred Macartney, recruited by Mackenzie for service in his organisation, not only wrote expansively and vividly on his period of intelligence work but was, notoriously, later prosecuted for treason.

So, it may be that the 'gentleman spy' was, at least in one sense, something of a misnomer and to define the term is a difficult task. Besides establishing details of background and other employment, there are also issues bearing on the precise nature of their involvement in intelligence work. Here it is useful to bear in mind some obvious points. Spies were, in the simplest terms, men engaged in covert information-gathering activities. Many spies merely undertook special duties as part of an otherwise mundane career; mundane, that is, by the standards of the day. Spies did not always remain spies for very long and evidential trails before or after their period in the secret world can sometimes be found. Some, such as the mysterious Mr Long, whose name appears on the Secret Service payrolls in the pre-1909 period, fell out of favour and lost their jobs. Having for several years acted in an operational capacity on the continent, on the outbreak of war Long found his application to become an officer blocked by his masters, who wished to have nothing more to do with him. The Irish novelist, Erskine Childers's interest in intelligence extended beyond the realms of fiction. He was himself involved in Naval Intelligence but only very briefly in 1916, and he quickly discovered that it was not for him. Most of the individuals featured in this book in fact had many occupations or posts in the course of their lives and all of them combined periods of active intelligence gathering with more sedentary intelligence analysis. Needless to say, relatively few ever advertised their activities afterwards.

Nor was their work invariably the stuff of a Buchan thriller. Relatively few who encountered the intelligence world did not have moments of danger and excitement but it was not necessarily the norm. In 1921, a British officer in Iraq noted of a fellow officer, Bradshawe, who was Secret Service Officer in Kirkuk, that he was the 'most bored man in Iraq' and that he spent his time 'resigning by every mail'. As mentioned previously, all the individuals in this book were, at times, actively involved in the hazardous business of gathering information abroad on behalf of the British government. However, they all shared experience of the less glamorous, deskbound, side of intelligence work. Paul Dukes, when recalled to London to liaise with the Foreign Office, remembered periods of intense frustration as he gazed out onto St James's Park from Room 7 of the Foreign Office. Yet, whether at the cutting edge of intelligence gathering or as one of what came to be known as the 'backroom boys', there was still a mystique about intelligence work, whatever its nature, which set its practitioners apart from those who might openly discuss their occupation.

In the early part of the twentieth century, British intelligence was still in the process of evolving into the various modern institutions of the State. Some intelligence bodies began to develop rapidly in the pre-war period and, more rapidly still, with the onset of war. However, in using the term 'gentleman spy' in this period, I would not wish to imply that British intelligence remained backward or amateurish. On the contrary, if current press reports were any indication, several of the individuals in this book would be the envy of their modern-day counterparts in their ability to pass unnoticed, but heavily disguised, in a crowded bazaar. Rather, this book attempts to investigate some of those unusual personalities whose intelligence-related activities reflected broader concerns about the safety of the empire and British interests, whether the dangers were posed by international conspiracies, conceived by the Bolsheviks, or by other rivals. On closer scrutiny, the world of John Buchan's Dick Hannay or the 'gay pursuit of a perilous quest' enjoyed by Erskine Childers's young Foreign Office man, Carruthers, was perhaps not entirely fanciful. Buchan invested his villains with great menace. Whether, it was the evil Scudder with his 'gimlety eyes', 'cold, malignant, unearthly, and most hellishly clever', or Barralty, or the uncomfortably realistic plot of *Greenmantle*, concerning an Islamic fundamentalist uprising, for many years the *bête noire* of the British India Office, there was invariably an evil genius, a single, controlling mind, seeking to thwart British interests. This fear was much to the fore in British analyses of threats to the empire during and after the First World War.

In tracing the activities of Britain's agents overseas, besides official papers, published works are also useful. Notable among these is Robert (later Baron Robert) Baden-Powell's *My Adventures as a Spy*. As he recalled, 'To be a really effective spy, a man has to be endowed with a strong spirit of self-sacrifice, courage, and self-control, with the power of acting a part, quick at observation and deduction, and blessed with good health and nerve of exceptional quality.' In a chapter entitled 'On the Cleverness of English Spies', Baden-Powell wrote ironically on 'the value of being stupid'. Although Germany's spies were, to a man, rounded up on the outbreak of war in 1914, this was not the case of their English counterparts: '. . . the exceedingly stupid

Englishman who wandered about foreign countries sketching cathedrals, or catching butterflies, or fishing for trout, were merely laughed at as harmless lunatics'. Had their drawings been subjected to scrutiny, the unsuspecting German officials would have found plans of their armaments and fortresses concealed among the pages of leaves or butterflies. In what amounted to a 'how-to' guide to espionage, Baden-Powell provided examples of quick disguises should the spy find himself in a tight corner. As he noted, spying brought a 'constant wearing strain of nerves and mind' but, in the father of scouting's experience, should all else fail, his motto had always held fast: 'a smile and a stick will carry you through any difficulty'.

The men chosen for intelligence gathering varied greatly. In its early stages, the Secret Service Bureau employed commercial travellers and businessmen as well as military personnel. The latter were mostly commissioned officers who, in wartime especially, were assigned to the intriguingly termed 'special duties'. For some this meant a desk job at the War Office or, less commonly, at the India Office or at the Admiralty. Their work was extremely diverse and encompassed everything from the preparation of political and economic intelligence summaries, to postal censorship, to the provision of information on particular areas of the world. Often they were paid little or nothing for this work and suffered uncomfortable working conditions. Some of these officers undoubtedly had special talents and some of them were civilians whose details cannot now be traced at all. Several of them had high linguistic abilities, whilst others had an academic or other background experience relevant to their wartime employment. More often, however, in the case of serving officers, they simply had a good education and were often recovering from a serious war injury that precluded active service.

In this group might be placed Norman Thwaites who, having been seriously injured at Messines, was asked by Sir William Wiseman, head of the British Secret Service in the United States during the war period, to go to New York and establish an intelligence branch. There, Thwaites gathered information on German spies and liaised closely with his American counterparts. With Sir Robert Nathan of the Indian Police, he also attempted to frustrate the machinations of anti-British Hindus, who hoped with German connivance to undermine British interests worldwide. Both Thwaites and Guy Gaunt, as Naval Attaché in the United States until March 1918, were also preoccupied with prominent German agents, who were doing everything to prevent the shipment of Allied goods to Europe. As Gaunt recalled in his memoirs, he was shadowed relentlessly whether he walked or drove. So frustrating did this become that he obtained a special pass that gave access to the foundations of a subway then under construction. This enabled him to shake off any pursuers and surface undetected several miles away.

A further casualty of war to be recruited to Britain's wartime intelligence operations was Captain G.A. Hill. In his memoirs, *Go Spy The Land*, Hill recalled that a knee injury received whilst on active service in France led to a posting to Military Intelligence at the War Office. There, after intensive training in all aspects of espionage, he was initially involved in counter-espionage work on the east coast of England. Afterwards, he was employed in the Balkans, in Egypt and then, from July 1917, in Russia. Hill was a remarkable man. Having mastered several languages as a boy and lived and travelled extensively in Russia, Persia and Central Asia, he was well suited to active intelligence work. He was a man of breathtaking daring. On one occasion, a passenger in the plane that he was piloting on an intelligence operation in the Balkans lost consciousness, thanks to his aerial stunts. In Russia, he developed a wide network of agents throughout northern and southern Russia and, like Paul Dukes, befriended the journalist Arthur Ransome, who, according to Hill, kept a pet snake in a large cigar box. Yet Hill was in no doubt about the qualities needed to be a spy. Above all he must be patriotic. Hill was himself on several occasions almost assassinated and as he stated, 'a spy carries his life in his hands'. He must have a 'brain of the utmost agility', capable of making a 'momentous decision in an instant'. To this he added a photographic memory and a genius for organising. For Hill, at least, his days in espionage 'were a joyful adventure'. Perhaps most important of all, however, whether or not they were recuperating from a war wound, recruits to the secret services knew someone who knew someone who had a brother who worked at the War Office . . . or something of that kind.

In the eastern Mediterranean theatre of the war there were equally talented and exotic British intelligence agents. We know that Compton Mackenzie's shadowy organisation, the Eastern Mediterranean Special Intelligence Bureau (EMSIB), cooperated with military intelligence in Egypt, and drew upon officers from across the services and both MI5 and MI1c to fill its ranks. Included among them were the brilliant linguist, author and traveller, Aubrey Herbert (the model for the Sandy Arbuthnott of Buchan's novels) and Lt Col Harry Pirie Gordon, the elusive officer of the Royal Naval Volunteer Reserve, who, with Herbert, was sent to gather intelligence in Alexandretta Bay in the autumn of 1914. Herbert went on to undertake a highly secret mission to Switzerland to investigate, on behalf of the British government, the possibility of a separate peace with Turkey. Though admired by many, some, including Lord Bertie of Thame, Britain's Ambassador in Paris, felt that Herbert's talents were not suited to political intelligence work. In October 1917, he demanded why Herbert, a 'dangerous pacifist Turcophile lunatic in khaki' was being allowed to roam about on such a mission. Similarly, Pirie Gordon, though a gallant and able intelligence officer, did not take well to the political duties that followed his period with Mackenzie. After a brief secondment to the Baltic as Deputy Political Commissioner there, he was relieved of this position, deemed too volatile and actually dangerous for such a sensitive position.

Wilfred Macartney's service under Mackenzie came as a relief from the dull existence of a censor. Of Mackenzie's base at Syra he noted: 'This was to be for nearly twelve months the centre from which I would set out to find adventure, peril, fun and love.' From Syra, Mackenzie, with the help of British officers and some Greek agents, controlled scores of islands, towns and harbours. Macartney's first mission was to secure the island paradise of Zea, by seizing its telephone and telegraph, its treasury and police station. With a map, a list of the island's inhabitants and their political affiliations, Macartney and an assortment of agents, all of them 'walking arsenals', accomplished the task with little opposition. Life there was pleasant. Besides his administrative and intelligence duties, Macartney found time for red mullet fishing, some game shooting and rounders, a form of baseball. There followed action-packed postings on missions which also involved members of the Whittall family and required courage and great physical stamina. On two occasions at least, Macartney found himself making night-time crossings of Greek islands to surprise opponents of Venizelos, the pro-Allied premier of Greece. There was a further posting to Amorgos, where, with the help of eight agents, Macartney again established a smooth administration. One of these agents, 'the famous Milton', was a 'big fat fellow of Levantine origin . . . with a most colourful past . . . a most egregious boaster, to me a most fascinating figure'. Among his other accomplishments, besides a finely honed ability to tell a story, Milton had captured the German diplomatic bag in Athens; something that Macartney was never allowed to forget. As Macartney recalled, he was the 'hush hush man of the cinema world of twenty years later'. As Mackenzie himself recounted, Macartney, at the age of a schoolboy, was himself the spy of the novel and of the screen.

Not everyone attached to Mackenzie's organisation experienced the thrill of 'ciphers, agents' reports, inter-departmental jealousies, international intrigues . . .' that made the period so exciting for Macartney. J.C. Lawson, a Cambridge don and RNVR officer, recalled his duties more soberly. The duty of a Naval Intelligence officer was, in his view, to liaise between his squadron and the population of the area to which he had been assigned. He translated, boarded vessels and examined cargo, and regulated anchorage in the vicinity of his squadron. He also liaised with the police, with the military and with diplomats. Yet even Lawson could not resist telling the tale of his part in apprehending the Bulgarian spy, Gatchieff. Whatever the truth, there were agents, runners and submarine watches to organise and life was seldom dull.

Gentleman Spies

The great upheavals in Russia during 1917 meant that intelligence about the country was in great demand and it is a subject on which professional historians and others have already written in some detail.* However, as political and intelligence-related material from the 1920s continues to be released, such research is ongoing and much has still to be yielded from the archives on, for example, the true story of Sidney Reilly, the engaging, enigmatic and brilliant agent who spied for Britain in Russia and elsewhere. Paul Dukes, whose story features in this work, was in many respects in the mould of a classic gentleman spy. Though from quite a different background, he rapidly proved himself to be an outstanding agent. Apart from his fluency in Russian, Dukes was blessed with an ability to substantially alter his appearance at short notice and obtain, by one means or another, the necessary papers and clothing to sustain each new identity. Sometimes, when travelling to and from Russia, Dukes would simply travel as a British officer, a Captain McNeill. On other occasions he and other agents adopted the guise of a 'King's Messenger' or courier, charged with the delivery of diplomatic and other despatches and materials between British possessions or representatives overseas.

---

* See, in particular, the article by Professor K. Neilson referred to in the Bibliography.

Ronald Sinclair, though no stranger to disguise, did not himself adopt that particular cover but some of his associates undoubtedly did. We know that one Colonel Treloar, with whom he worked in the refugee camps around Constantinople in 1920 and who also had intelligence-gathering functions, occupied just such a position. Similarly, the mysterious Albert Stopford, who operated in Russia for several years, regularly visited Russia in the capacity of courier. So well established was it as a cover in espionage operations that, in the world of fiction, Buchan's Sandy Arbuthnott adopted that disguise, before disappearing as a 'queer Oriental ruffian' in Cairo.

Dukes's story is recounted from his books, *Red Dusk and The Morrow* (1922) and *The Story of 'ST 25'* (1938), from archive material in public and private collections, and from several newspapers. This second work was in January 1941 referred to by Leo Amery, Secretary of State for India, as 'perhaps the best true spy story of our time'. The researcher, as is often the case with official papers, is often helped by the unwillingness of government departments to dispose of papers that touch on their financial obligations. In Dukes's case, this has made possible the identification of some of his collaborators among surviving Foreign Office documents. We know, for example, that one of Dukes's most able collaborators was a British man of the name John Merrett or Merritt, whose work for British interests in Russia left the British Government long indebted to him.

Dukes had been preceded in Russia by Samuel (later Sir Samuel) Hoare. Like Dukes, his induction to the mysteries of the Secret Service had begun with a meeting with Sir Mansfield Cumming. To Hoare he was 'in all respects, physical and mental, the antithesis of the spy king of popular fiction. Jovial and very human, bluff and plain speaking, outwardly at least, a very simple man. . . .' As with Dukes, too, an intensive training in the arts of espionage, counter-espionage, coding and cyphering, war trade and contraband, postal and telegraphic, also preceded it. In fact, after his period of Secret Service work in Russia, Hoare went on to head the SIS mission in Italy and saw further service in Ireland. Hoare recalled of his work that much of it was indeed mundane and consisted of the signalling of the whereabouts of suspect persons, intercepting contraband, transmitting reports and analysing departmental memoranda. Occasionally, a piece of high-quality material would emerge and he would transmit it to his political masters in London. Unlike Dukes, who spent most of his time living in disguise and in constant fear of the Russian secret police, Hoare was an accredited officer and an MP, something that greatly assisted his information-gathering efforts among Russian politicians. Above all, Dukes was an important spy because the information that he supplied was quite unique. He was able to obtain it for such a long time because of his ability to disguise himself and to ingratiate himself with and gain the trust of many different groups and individuals. His experience of espionage was highly dangerous and, had he been detected, he might at any time have been shot.

The nature of intelligence gathering in Britain's colonial possessions has yet to be systematically analysed and, in Chapter 3, an episode from this story is recounted. The outbreak of war with Turkey in the autumn of 1914 meant that Britain's large Muslim population had to be watched very closely. In his 1916 novel *Greenmantle*, John Buchan's character, Dick Hannay, listened intently as Sir Walter Bullivant of the Foreign Office told him of the 'dry wind blowing through the East'. Concerns about subversive movements were widespread among officials in Britain, India and other outposts of empire. Among other fears, they felt that extreme Muslims would seek to undermine British rule. Worse still, German agents and those of other European nations would seek to stoke up resentment among the Muslim population. This was an important strand of British high policy in the Middle East and Central Asia. It was also significant in Muslim North Africa, where the memory of General Gordon's murder was still relatively fresh. During and immediately after the First World War there had been concerns about the activities of various groups that might become hostile to British interests. These included pan-Islamists, organisations planning for a 'vast Negro Republic in Africa', and the resurgence of Mahdism. The savage giant, Colonel von Stumm, with whom Dick Hannay grapples in *Greenmantle*, told him to 'find the race that fears its priests' – the 'Mussulmans of Somaliland and the Abyssinian Border and the Blue and White Nile'. Stumm continues, 'they would be like dried grasses to catch fire if you used the flint and steel of their religion'. Often, as we shall also see in Chapter 4, fears of such currents were ill-defined and merged into what might today be termed conspiracy theory. Officials in Whitehall, Simla and other far-flung posts of empire struggled to understand these movements and generally failed. Comparisons were made between Muslim religious movements and Welsh revivalists or, in terms of their organisational structures, the Synod of the Church of Scotland. Yet the problems faced in understanding those movements were great. Often fragmented intelligence had to be pieced together and it was difficult then as it is now to attach appropriate value to material that might indicate connections, loose or otherwise, between hostile elements. In the case of the investigations undertaken by Herbert, later Sir Herbert, Palmer (1877–1958) and Gordon, later Sir Gordon, Lethem (1886–1962), explored in Chapter 3, senior officials in Whitehall also detected a single source, a 'central brain', behind this evil. This tied in closely with broader fears, expressed by many political, military and intelligence officials. There was also difficulty in establishing the parameters of the unrest. Some officials were inclined to be dismissive of those who, like Lethem, were sensitive to its possibly hostile intentions. Yet the unrest did exist and whether, as in the case of Morocco, it was referred to as 'nationalism' or as a 'revolt against civilisation', or if, as in other countries, it had a religious aspect, it had to be investigated.

At an institutional level, during the First World War, MI5 and its precursor had begun to develop parallel organisations in the British colonies. After the war, and during the 1920s, greater efforts were made to consider the colonial dimension when gathering intelligence about threats within or beyond the empire. To this end, several meetings took place between MI5, SIS, Scotland Yard and the Colonial Office, to consider how best to coordinate their activities.

For those who might wish to follow up my research on Nigeria, I have drawn upon many Colonial and Foreign Office documents, private collections, national newspapers and scholarly articles. Palmer's report is held at the PRO under reference CO 583/83. Lethem's report was not finally completed and printed until 1927. Then, it was accompanied by a further memorandum by G.J. Tomlinson, and was entitled *History of Islamic Political Propaganda in Nigeria* and ran to two volumes. A further volume that Lethem appears to have envisaged and which was to be composed from his edited diaries (which extend to over four hundred pages) was never completed. The final version of the report may be seen among Lethem's papers at Rhodes House Library in Oxford. A draft version is available at the PRO at CO 583/138. The Foreign and Commonwealth Library also holds a copy.

For Lethem at least, his intelligence duties were simply an interesting episode in a long and successful career in the Colonial Service, which he had entered with a law degree from Edinburgh University. After service in Nigeria he obtained several colonial governorships, the last in British Guyana from 1941 to 1946, and subsequently became Vice-President of the Scottish Liberal Party. Palmer remained in the Nigerian Service, having been recommended for a CBE for his work in investigating the Mahdist threat.

In the case of Reginald Teague-Jones, or Ronald Sinclair as he was known from about 1922, my research has been assisted by his longevity and his long-term involvement in intelligence work of one kind or another. Jones/Sinclair was born in 1889 and maintained an interest in world affairs and apparently gathered intelligence formally or otherwise into the 1960s. He has left an extensive archive that is split between the Oriental and India Office Collections of the British Library and the Imperial War Museum. Peter Hopkirk, the author of many excellent books on the Great Game, has edited the diaries that Sinclair kept during his period of service in Transcaspia at the end of the First World War and I have drawn on this material in Chapter 1. More concentrated searches at the PRO and other archives have helped to reveal further important details from this period and from his later life. I have also based my account upon Sinclair's book *Travels in Persia*. Sinclair was an avid note-taker and writer and contributed many articles to journals during the 1920s and 1930s. When he died in 1988 he was apparently working on the publication of a further book. He spent little time in England and, as one magazine article noted, he was cursed or blessed with 'an unusually virulent form of "wanderlust"'.

Besides Sinclair's period of intelligence duties in Transcaspia and then in and around Constantinople and the Black Sea, in an earlier period both he and Ely Soane, whose story appears in Chapter 2, had undertaken periods of active intelligence work tracking down the notorious German spy Wassmuss. The activities of that individual, fomenting anti-British sentiments on the Persian–Mesopotamian frontier, had caused great concern among the British authorities. Soane, Sinclair, and other intelligence officers such as the indefatigable Major Edward Noel, tried in vain to capture the elusive spy.

To appreciate the scale of Sinclair's achievements, one must realise the nature of the Transcaspian region where he spent a crucial part of his career. Little known to British people other than in stories of the Old Silk Road, it was desperately inaccessible and remote. Furthermore, in terms of the higher direction of the war, the British Cabinet had failed properly to unify British command or intelligence gathering there or, indeed, anywhere in Central Asia or the Middle East. For six months, however, Sinclair, who was barely in his thirtieth year, ran the Transcaspian government. Admittedly his background had prepared him well for this. His language skills, his physical fitness, and his political astuteness were indispensable but nothing could really have prepared him for the complexities that faced him. Not only had he to deal with personal danger but also with repeated requests from the local population for the British government to come to their aid when it was clear to him that they had no such intention. In the case of Norman Bray, whose story appears in Chapter 4, this duplicity was too much. He felt that the Arabs had been misled by the British government and for that reason he resigned one of his special military intelligence appointments. As for Sinclair, one cannot read his accounts of physical stamina and daring, both in Transcaspia and in Persia in the mid-1920s, without feeling intense admiration. He was utterly determined in the face of extreme adversity and his exploits were on occasion quite breathtaking.

We have already noted the concerns arising from Britain's conflict with the Ottoman Empire. It was chiefly in this context that Norman Bray played his part in the intelligence world. In several capacities, he investigated and analysed the various threats to Britain's eastern empire. By 1919, when his work began in earnest, many officials were gripped by fears of hostile conspiracies. These were not seen in isolation but, as a result of information supplied by SIS and by other sources, they rapidly developed into a vast and hostile coalition of forces that extended throughout the empire, England included, and beyond. Concern soon became apparent at the Foreign Office. To Sir Eyre Crowe, Assistant Under Secretary of State, the Jews were chiefly to blame. In his view they were in league with the Bolsheviks and the Turkish Committee of Union and Progress (CUP), and were together 'the heart and soul of all revolutionary and terroristic movements'. George Kidston, also of the Foreign Office, was particularly alarmed. On receiving M.H. Kidwai's work, *The Sword Against Islam*, Kidston noted that Kidwai was 'the most notorious of the Woking Mosque Gang', which was 'in common with all the most dangerous conspirators in this country and abroad'. The book was, in Kidston's view, 'poisonous stuff but diabolically clever'. He continued: 'it is the gospel of the latest form of CUP Bolshevism directed against the British Empire more especially in India and Egypt. It shows more clearly than anything I have seen yet how this movement is connected up with every form of revolutionary activity throughout the world: CUP, Bolshevism, Indian and Egyptian nationalism, anti-Zionism, Sinn Fein, the extreme Labour Party, Japanese Asiaticism, [and] Persian "democracy".' Similarly, in January 1920, Colin Garbett of the India Office, when commenting on a memorandum by Bray on 'pan-Orientalism', noted that whilst it was a model of its kind and should be circulated both to secret service agencies and to Mesopotamia for the guidance of political officers there, it failed properly to address the rôle of the United States in stirring up discontent.

Assessments of this kind were based upon the collective effect of reports gathered at listening posts in Europe, Asia and in the United States and Canada by a wide variety of individuals. Such reports are now scattered chiefly among Foreign Office documents and those of the Political and Secret, and Public and Judicial Departments of the India Office. Relatively few, however, offer anything more than fragments of intelligence rather than a broader assessment of these threats as they developed in the Middle East and Central Asia. It was to this task that Bray devoted himself, having personally investigated the nature of the threat. From the India Office he had access to many intelligence sources including reports from SIS, from MI5, from several other sections of military intelligence, from the Indian Political Police, from the Admiralty, Foreign Office and from Director of Special Intelligence, Sir Basil Thomson. A fresh analysis of his life has been made possible by the chance discovery at the PRO of a long and fascinating autobiographical account that Bray submitted to the King during the Second World War in support of a claim that he had been unfairly denied a position in the Middle East.

Chapter 2 tells the story of Ely Soane (1881–1923), whose colourful life I have pieced together from wide-ranging archival sources and material written by Soane himself. In particular, besides several of his articles and books on Kurdish language and society, I have drawn on his book, *To Mesopotamia and Kurdistan in Disguise*, published in 1912. Of course, Soane was not the first English traveller to venture into the Arab Middle East in disguise. Well before his time, William Palgrave had traversed the Arabian Peninsula and become the first European to visit Riyadh. He managed to do so by disguising himself variously as a priest, a Jesuit, a missionary and a doctor.

In fact, at least a dozen other British travellers, most of them Army officers, had visited parts of Kurdistan prior to Soane's arrival there in 1909. Soane's attraction lies in the fact that he wrote vividly and authoritatively on the Kurdish language and culture, that he journeyed as a 'way of escape' and out of sheer 'curiosity'. He was a man who was happiest and perhaps only ever really happy when in the wildest parts of Kurdistan or Persia. Also, although his official intelligence-gathering duties were undertaken in a relatively short space of time, Soane was in many ways typical – if one so eccentric can be so described – of the kind of gentleman traveller who provided information to the British government. In Soane's case, it was not butterfly collecting or a desire to paint that spurred him on to explore and record what he saw. Rather, it was innate curiosity and the love and fascination for a people, 'high-spirited and quick-witted, physically superior and doggedly independent', whom he felt had been neglected and undervalued by European civilisation. Yet at the time there was considerable confusion in Whitehall and among British authorities in the Middle East, as to the purpose of his journey. Some alleged that he was travelling on behalf of an 'oriental society', whilst a mission on behalf of the British Museum was also suggested. In retrospect, Soane claimed that, before embarking on his journey, he had no intention of producing a report. He sought only 'linguistic, ethnological and historical information'. He went in disguise mainly to ensure 'access to every class of Kurd', to gain 'unhampered passage through their country and the close intercourse, which alone confers familiarity with a people's language'. Such was Soane's fluency in the Persian language and his linguistic skills in general that he could assimilate with just about any nationality. Further, he was physically and mentally resilient, brave, and willing to risk his life, sometimes without any particularly good reason. All of these qualities were essential in the huge triangle of territory – all 95,000 square miles of mainly mountainous and wild country – that Soane called Kurdistan. He was also immensely adaptable in his ability to undertake all manner of occupations – engineer, accountant, banker, newspaper editor and intelligence officer – and all of them, it seems, with some ability. It is also likely that he retained some of the acting skills that had distinguished him as a schoolboy, for in the course of his career he was frequently called upon to adopt many disguises to avoid difficult situations. Like many others who have been drawn to the world of intelligence, his brilliant nature included a wayward streak that at times brought him into conflict with his superiors. Yet he was outstanding in his ability to pass himself off as a native of Persia and of Kurdistan and to sustain these disguises when subjected to all but the closest scrutiny.

The search for information on William Childs, whose travels are described in Chapter 5, became something of a personal crusade. I first encountered him, or rather his initials, or, to be precise, those that he most commonly used, appended to a Foreign Office memorandum written in the 1920s. Further searches revealed that he had journeyed across Turkey in the early years of the twentieth century and that he had recorded details of his journey in a travel book. An analysis of this text and of the Foreign Office memorandum, which focused on the pan-Turkish movement and its significance during the First World War, suggested that he was no regular diplomat. Indeed, the timing of the memorandum, quite apart from its contents, coinciding as it did with further intelligence-gathering efforts in the Turkish interior, pointed to the possibility that Childs himself had been gathering intelligence as he travelled. In fact, the more I researched Childs's life and experienced difficulty in finding information, the more intriguing it became. Although Childs claimed to be a British passport holder, I was unable to find reference to a birth certificate. Indeed, whichever way my research turned, I could find no real leads pointing to his personal history prior to his first period of residence in Turkey. A subsequent discovery that he may have held the rank of Captain, seemed to offer hope. His journey, in terms of its duration, appeared to correspond to previous travels across Asia Minor by Army officers on extended leave or half-pay. Yet Childs's name does not appear among copies of half-pay registers at the PRO, or, more importantly, among copies of the *Army List*. A further glimmer of hope lay in the possibility that, like some other officers awaiting promotion or a staff appointment, Childs had been seconded to the Ottoman Gendarmerie. Such a position, as with a civil attachment to a department of the Turkish government, would have afforded Childs scope to observe. In particular, I sought to understand his insights into the influence upon Turkish soldiers and others of their German counterparts, whose activities in pre-war Turkey he had witnessed. A similar search among equivalent Royal Navy records suggested that he was neither a naval officer, attached to the British Naval Mission in Constantinople, nor an Admiralty 'reporting officer' there. Nor, it seems, according to my extensive searches, was he of the Royal Marines, British Merchant Marine, Royal Naval Reserve or the Legion of Frontiersmen. Also precluded by my research were the Indian Army and the Honourable Artillery Company. Nor was he, it seems, a schoolmaster. A business connection or cover seemed possible but I was unable to link him to any specific British concern in Turkey in that period.

As to a possible consular appointment, this too seemed likely at first. The volumes of consular and general correspondence for pre-war Ottoman Turkey were fascinating and helpful in my efforts to understand the nature and scope of British interests in the region. They were also useful in trying to identify a British Consular official who accompanied Childs on part of his journey and for whom Childs appeared to have a very exalted, almost reverential, opinion. I was intrigued to find that the Foreign Office had insisted on such escorts as a general rule for travellers in this region. Yet a search of these Foreign Office documents and of Treasury documents ruled out the possibility of a consular appointment.

There could be no doubt that the War Office, especially, was keen to gather information on the Turkish interior at this time. We know that Britain employed agents in pre-war Turkey. Constantinople, as the crossroads of two continents and as a melting pot for many races, was a perfect listening post not only for information on Turkish affairs, but also the interests and aspirations of Britain's European rivals. In June 1911, the Director of Military Operations refused the offer of information on the Alexandretta basin, a vital strategic position, from a staff officer based in Cairo, on the grounds that the Foreign Office would not 'entertain the idea'. Quite simply, in the aftermath of the Armenian massacres and of the war between Italy and Turkey, it was too dangerous. More importantly, however, the letter continued:

> As a matter of fact we have had a very useful report, from another source, not only about the place itself, but about the influence – German and other – which is at work both at the port and in the surrounding country, so we are for the moment, at any rate, up to date in our knowledge of what is going on there.

Such hints of Childs's earlier handiwork encouraged lengthy forays among official papers, and my research also took me to the private collections of many officials across the country in the hope of discovering further clues. Some of these officials, especially those who served in Turkey when Childs lived and travelled there, also left memoirs in published or manuscript form, yet none of them mention him by name. Nor, indeed, was he traceable in the several detailed theses which have been written on aspects of the British presence in Turkey and which are based on extensive trawls of many archival sources.

Nor could I find a link between Childs and the emerging commercial intelligence community. Research on this area has been much neglected, partly because relatively few of the files of the Commercial Intelligence Department of the Board of Trade have survived. The evolution of this department, in tandem with reporting arrangements for British Consuls overseas, seemed a suitable context for Childs's information gathering; yet, it seems, they did not employ him.

Such information as I did obtain about Childs, related almost exclusively to the war or postwar period and only then after exhaustive and speculative research among official directories, membership lists for prominent learned societies, and probate and General Register Office sources. Indeed, it was only in the period of postwar retrenchment that Childs emerges from the shadows of official papers. In the 1920s, in various temporary posts with Naval Intelligence or with the Foreign Office, which the Treasury was eager to abolish, the once active intelligence gatherer was required to provide detailed analyses of the various regions of which he had experience. Then we find Childs contributing steadily to discussions about the Balkans, the Arab Middle East, Cyprus and the Caucasus. Yet few, in fact very few, of the collections of papers of individuals with whom he must have had some official dealings, contain any mention of him. When they do they are unusually discreet and so brief as to arouse instant suspicion. Typically, we know that Childs worked in Room 4 of the Foreign Office where he, and fellow workers, assembled a mass of information on the Near and Middle East. Beyond this, however, questions remain about Childs's identity. He died in 1933 and, although married, and whilst his wife outlived him by several decades, he had no children and she, it seems, left her belongings to charity or to a niece who cannot now be traced. Of his schooling and any subsequent education, my extensive searches have revealed nothing. In many ways, it seems, William Childs was the quintessential gentleman spy, elusive to the last.

Missions and Debriefings

Fooling a German sentry (found near a rifle range)

1

A Blanket, a Haversack and Flour for Chapattis

ON THE FRONTIERS OF AFGHANISTAN

In the first years of the twentieth century, in St Petersburg, a small English boy puzzled at a commotion in front of his carriage as he tried to cross the city. His mind gripped by the possibility of excitement and adventure – he had just been reading G.A. Henty – he descended from the carriage. This was the rumoured outbreak happening in front of his eyes. Thrilled with the prospect of glimpsing the Tsar and demonstrations outside the Winter Palace, suddenly he sensed panic in the air. People began to stampede. The police opened fire and, as the boy recalled in later life, 'I experienced the feelings of a bullock that has just scented the slaughterhouse'. In a moment he was caught up by the crowd, driven down by mounted Cossacks, and found himself knocked into the gutter with cuts to his head. So intoxicating was that sense of danger that the boy, and later the man, Reginald Teague-Jones, was destined to lead a life on the edge; a life of intrigue spent almost exclusively overseas and much of it in the world of secret intelligence.

Some years later, after a spell at university in London, the same adventurous spirit had found a suitable niche with a commission in the Indian frontier police. There, with a small group of handpicked men, he patrolled the North-West Frontier, ensuring that unruly tribes were duly brought to account. In a town called Tonk, unbearably hot and malaria-ridden, an exotic outpost of carpets, skins, fruits, nuts and spices, Jones recalled a 'tough and hazardous life, calling for and producing extreme physical fitness'. At Tonk and later, when stationed at Nishpa, Jones's life was alternately

35

monotonous and wildly exciting. As he breakfasted on tea laced with whisky, wrapped in his British Warm overcoat, he would listen to Harry Lauder's 'The Braes of Killiecrankie' on an ancient gramophone; a *Jamadar* occasionally nudging the sticking needle. Amid a din of human voices, crowing roosters, and the braying of donkeys, Jones passed the time reading Turgenev's *Notes of a Hunter* and another work, *Campaigns on the North West Frontier*. More significantly, perhaps, for his later life, Jones also studied his Persian Grammar. Having obtained his Higher Standard in the language, he now worked towards his Proficiency Persian exam. A gun was never far from his reach and he slept with a revolver under his pillow. Sometimes his night-time routines were punctuated by midnight forays in search of raiding parties. Equipped only with a blanket, haversack, water bottle and first-aid kit, his patrol would carry only the barest supplies of flour for chapattis, some chickpeas and a lump of *goor*. On this basic diet, they would march anything between twenty and fifty miles a day, 'toiling through ravines, exploring *nullahs* and climbing summits'. They moved carefully, never without posting advance scouts and, ever fearful of ambush, would never linger around a campfire or water hole.

This apprenticeship in fieldcraft was invaluable experience for a subsequent posting to the Persian Gulf as Intelligence Officer. There, Jones was personally instructed by the Commander in Chief at Simla, General Kirkpatrick, to capture the notorious German agent Wassmuss. So vital was this objective, that Jones was instructed to take him 'dead or alive'. Though Jones never did capture the elusive and highly skilled agent, he did entrap his right-hand man, Bruggmann, and, though clearly of little comfort to Jones's superiors, recovered Wassmuss's atlas.*

---

* Sinclair's lack of success might be excused. Wassmuss was fluent in English and Persian and was a master of disguise, on occasion adopting the appearance of a donkey-man and even an elderly Persian woman. When pursued by Sinclair he converted to Islam and lived as a Kashgai tribesman. One officer of the South Persia Force remembered him as a 'brave man who gave us a lot of trouble, and served his country well'.

Some months later, in June 1918, a group of senior politicians and military personnel met in secret conclave at the House of Commons. The discussion of this group, the War Cabinet's secret Eastern Committee, turned on events in Afghanistan and Central Asia. More specifically, Sir Henry Wilson, the Chief of the Imperial General Staff, a tall and calculating Ulsterman, expressed the fears of the War Office that the northern frontier of Afghanistan was again exposed to enemy penetration. As Wilson intoned, German and Turkish forces were approaching the Caspian and the disintegration of the Russian military and political situation added further uncertainty. The 'German wave' was 'sweeping over the Don Basin towards the Volga'. In the Trans-Caucasus, German troops held Tiflis and their advance on Baku was imminent. German agents were already active in Tashkent, spreading rumours as to the impending arrival of the German Army.

* * *

Earlier in 1918, the India Office had taken a preliminary step towards despatching a mission to Turkestan. Bases had been established at Meshed and Kashgar but neither party was permitted to enter Russian-controlled territory. Politicians were concerned by the prospect of military action on the Afghan frontier and neighbouring Khanates. Experience showed that it did not pay to meddle there. They were also deeply concerned at the possibility of military action in so remote and inaccessible a place. The War Office had already pushed an expedition under General Dunsterville into north-west Persia, ostensibly to block the easterly movement of the Turkish–German forces. Now there was every sign that this cordon was insufficient and that enemy forces would cross the Caspian and march on India. The War Office, especially, was forceful in pressing for intelligence officers at Meshed and Kashgar to be allowed to cross into Turkestan. From Meshed, it was hoped that officers would work up friendly elements in Transcaspia and destroy the Transcaspian railway, from which Germany hoped to launch an attack on India. There, these officers might also gather information about the Orenburg–Tashkent railway and the forty thousand Austrian and German prisoners of war who only required food and supplies in order to become a further potentially hostile force in the region. Also, there was the rumoured purchase by Germany of massive supplies of raw cotton in Turkestan, which the mission must at all costs prevent from reaching Europe. It was in response to these dangerous developments that Captain Teague-Jones and his fellow officer, Captain Jarvis, formerly an engineer in Russia, slipped quietly into Turkestan. At about the same time, instructions were sent to General Marshall in Mesopotamia, to despatch a party to Krasnovodsk in an attempt to gain control of shipping on the Caspian.

Jones's passage from Simla to Meshed took him forty days. En route, besides being involved in a serious train accident, he encountered fellow officers bound for Meshed. At Dalbadin, he learned that a Major Bingham was only ten days' march ahead and was also bound for Meshed. Bingham, whom Jones knew slightly, was a well-known panicmonger and had been spreading wild rumours about the imminent fall of Turkestan to the enemy. He was also of the school that liked to travel well prepared; and, on this occasion, caused Jones much amusement by having no fewer than twelve regulation camel-loads of gear. At Robat, Jones also encountered a thoroughly obstinate Commanding Officer in General Dale and another, highly eccentric, fellow officer in Lieutenant Ward, who had apparently arrived with rather mysterious instructions from the War Office. To Jones, at any rate, Ward seemed – apart from being a very 'gallant fellow' – to be quite out of his depth, lacking even a basic understanding of Persian, and dangerously ill-equipped for such a challenging journey. Robat itself, Jones considered a 'pestilential, Godforsaken spot', not only because of its Commanding Officer but also because of the plague of flies which afflicted it.

Having arrived safely in Meshed, Jones learned more of the enigmatic Ward from the Military Attaché, Colonel Redl. Apparently, Ward had presented himself at the Russian section of the War Office Intelligence Department and had inveigled them into sponsoring him on a mission to blow up a major bridge on the railway between Krasnovodsk and Askhabad. As Jones recorded in his diary, no one had bothered to test Ward's claims to be practised in the use of explosives and he was 'accordingly despatched with War Office blessing right round the world via Canada and Japan so that no one would suspect that his ultimate destination was Turkistan'. Unfortunately, as Jones continued, in Montreal Ward received a letter addressed: 'Lt K Ward, en route Turkistan, Montreal'. His cover was well and truly blown.

In Meshed itself, Jones and Ward realised how little Colonel Redl or the Consul-General, Colonel Grey, who cordially loathed one another, actually knew or cared about events in Turkestan. At once, Jones began to assess the likelihood of groups in the local population assisting his plans to penetrate into Transcaspia. Having considered enlisting Armenian or Kurdish help, he decided against both and instead resolved to slip into Turkestan in disguise. Jarvis had already done so but nothing had been heard of him. As Jones noted, he had used disguise before and both he and Gulab Hussein, his Indian travelling companion, were fluent enough in Persian to support his guise as a 'sort of Persian Armenian trader'. In this disguise, his coat lining stuffed with rouble notes and bearing a tin uniform box to test the feasibility of later smuggling explosives, Jones and Gulab Hussein set out. Jarvis, as Jones discovered when they met soon afterwards, had reached Askhabad only to find that the Bolshevik authorities there were obviously sympathetic towards the Germans and Turks. Rumours of enemy propaganda were borne out by Jarvis's experience, as were German plans for trans-shipping cotton supplies. It was to the frustration of this plan from Krasnovodsk that Jones turned his attention, as he recorded in his diary:

From now onwards I began to dream of cotton. I saw myself arriving at Krasnovodsk to find trainloads of cotton lying down by the docks and saw myself with Gulab Hussein pouring oil on it and setting fire to it by night. I developed this idea until I saw myself destroying the entire port of Krasnovodsk by fire and decided that if necessary I would do this and thus render the destruction of the bridge and all the trouble with explosives unnecessary. Henceforth I went on with the journey feeling that at last I had something definite and practical in view and that my visit to Transcaspia would have more far reaching results than I had at first anticipated.

Though nervous about encountering his first Bolshevik-controlled frontier crossing, Jones was allowed to pass and, with only physical discomfort due to an overcrowded train and a distinct lack of food, he safely reached Krasnovodsk on the Caspian Sea. Jones recalled his emotions on first reaching Central Asia:

The sun was now already well above the horizon and its rays lit up the distant Persian hills and glistened on the shining steel rails that seemed an incongruous and intrusive imposition thrust upon this primitive landscape. So this was the famous Central Asian Railway.

The railway itself was disappointing but Jones found that the region as a whole quite lived up to his boyhood dreams and, as he awaited the daily train with Gulab Hussein, he conjured with visions of the Old Silk Road wending towards Merv, Bokhara, Samarkand and Tashkent. The arrival of the train and the need to satisfy his hunger in the station buffet before its departure ended these musings with a jolt. As Jones remarked, here was a scene from a London musical comedy:

There were Russian peasants in red shirts, Armenians and Persians, Cossacks and Red soldiers, Sart traders and Bokhariots,

Turkmans in their gigantic *papakhas*, while among the crowd were a number of pretty young girls and women in the latest Paris summer fashions. All this medley came crushing into the buffet and clamoured for glasses of tea, hunks of black bread and platters of soup. Somehow or other they all seemed to get served and Asiatic and European, Mongol and Muscovite sat down literally cheek by jowl, and satisfied their hunger.

By the time of his arrival in Baku several days later, Jones had been without proper food for five days, had endured a search of his luggage – ironically enough on suspicion that he might be carrying bombs – and had undergone a severe crossing of the Caspian Sea which left him seasick and with sunstroke. Having regained his composure, consumed four large omelettes and bought himself a straw hat, Jones set out to investigate the situation.

According to Major MacDonell, the British Consul at Baku, the Turks were then only forty miles from the city and were intent on its capture. The various factions in the city – Bolsheviks, Centro-Caspian Directorate, Armenians, the Caspian Fleet and the anti-Bolsheviks – were unwilling to unite against the Turks and the Bolsheviks appeared actively to be preventing action against them. 'Dunsterforce', the British force under the command of General Dunsterville, was unable to reach Baku and could not therefore relieve the situation. Baku was cut off from the rest of the Caucasus and from communications with the British authorities either in Mesopotamia or Persia. Armed with this most recent picture of the situation, Jones resolved to return to Meshed 'in record time'. It was vital to communicate this information to his superiors without delay.

In this brief foray into the Caucasus, Jones displayed many of the hallmarks of a successful intelligence agent. A master of several languages including Persian, Russian and Hindi, he was able to converse with many types of people and, due to his persuasive charm, gain their confidence. He was also, as we shall see, a highly capable administrator, with an equally high degree of diplomacy, who never lost sight of the broader political picture. He was also physically fit, tough, quick-thinking and, although he didn't realise it at the time, several of these qualities were to be essential on his return to Meshed.

On his outward journey, Jones had noticed large quantities of cotton stacked on the railway line between Kaakha and Krasnovodsk and there were already further substantial stores at the latter place. He had also learned of the existence at Astrakhan on the northern shores of the Caspian of a German mission whose aim was to trans-ship this cotton across the Caspian. The issue had already caused great concern at the India Office and had been discussed by the Eastern Committee. It had been proposed to put the cotton out of reach of the enemy by transporting it to Kashgar at a total cost of roughly one and a half million pounds. On his return to Krasnovodsk en route for Meshed, Jones realised that the cotton was now being loaded onto vessels. With great haste and presence of mind, having enlisted the help of some local associates (whose names he deliberately altered to protect their identity), Jones ensured it was never sent. Mysteriously, the Krasnovodsk Executive Committee, which had collaborated in the shipping, received a wireless message, apparently from Astrakhan but in fact from Jones's associate, insisting that the vessels be unloaded and all other spare craft be sent to Petrovsk to carry vital supplies. As Jones later pointed out, although he had personally engineered the entire operation, he was never officially thanked for it.

From Krasnovodsk Jones took a train to Askhabad, apparently succumbing to the charms of a female passenger and a conveniently located rear platform on the train, to ensure that his night-time scanning of the passing countryside for sign of Ward's bridge did not arouse the suspicions of the train attendant. Through Askhabad, which he found in chaos and suspense as a result of a recent coup, he continued to Kaakha, then embarking with mules and a reluctant muleteer for a breakneck race to

Meshed. His party, having been set upon by dogs at the frontier, was detained by the border guards and only with a good deal of persuasion and cajoling, were they at last allowed to proceed towards the mountains. Against all advice, Jones insisted on a night-time crossing and soon found his face 'cut to cracks' by the biting and freezing wind. After further superhuman exertions, Jones arrived late the following night at the 'black and jagged silhouette' of the city walls. Unable to find an entrance in the dark, he dragged and half carried his exhausted mule across a deep ditch – unfortunately used by the Meshedis as a waste tip – broke through a wall and was finally escorted to the British Consulate by a posse of indignant Persians. There, as he recalled, the urgency of the situation was quite lost on Jarvis, Redl, Bingham and, most of all, and to Jones's intense irritation, on General Malleson, who was then asleep and who had recently been appointed to head the Meshed Mission.

Jones was disappointed by Malleson and Redl's apparent lack of understanding of the situation. However, all were agreed that further information was required about the situation in Askhabad and Jones volunteered for a further mission. As he recalled, though desperately in need of rest, the idea of the trip 'enthralled me'. Having renewed his acquaintance with Ward – whose bridge was now known not to exist – the two men left Meshed, disguised as traders.

In Askhabad, Jones lost no time in meeting the leaders of the recent coup: Dokhor, 'lean and slovenly . . . with a hungry look about him and a shifty glint in his eye'; Funtikov, 'thick-set and flabby'; and the weaselly Kurilev. The 'Askhabad Committee' as they called themselves clearly wished for instant British assistance but, unlike the British, their aim was principally to avoid Bolshevik retribution rather than defeat the Turkish advance. Having proceeded to Baku, Jones found the city in upheaval and panic and its fall to the Turks was imminent. Ward, despite his inadequacies as an explosives officer, had in the meantime obtained a large-scale map of the defences of the city and Jones, under strict orders to acquire just such a map, though risking certain death if it were found on his person, managed to exfiltrate it through port customs by folding it in a newspaper under his arm. This, and some equally quick thinking when a communist soldier challenged him as he awaited the departure of his vessel for Krasnovodsk, saved his skin.

After a further sojourn in Baku, with the Turkish threat now momentarily receding, Jones took up intelligence duties under the command of General Dunsterville. This, and further service in Transcaspia, enabled him to build up networks of agents across the region. This work was interrupted suddenly when he received orders to return immediately to Askhabad. Bolshevik troops had invaded Transcaspia. At Kaakha, Jones learned that the Bolsheviks had renewed the attack and that they outnumbered the British by three to one. On 28 August he personally led a counterattack in which he was wounded and Ward, for whom Jones now had some affection and regard, fatally so.

Although this episode marked a temporary end to Jones's physical exertions, his appointment for five months as Political Representative to Transcaspia meant that he was now the sole conduit between the Askhabad Committee and General Malleson in Meshed. The Askhabad Committee had in the meantime reorganised itself with Funtikov at its head. As Jones recalled, in earlier life Funtikov had been an engine driver:

> In his proper sphere of life he had no doubt been a very worthy fellow and when sober probably a very good engine driver, but he was no earthly use as a Prime Minister. He was very crude in his manners, extremely illiterate, but like so many of his kidney, painfully verbose and pretended to a certain skill in cheap rhetoric, so dear to all revolutionaries, particularly in Russia. His greatest weakness was drink, and although vodka and other strong beverages were supposed to be taboo, nevertheless, Funtikov – F-F-Funtikov as we generally called him, and he not infrequently called himself – was very rarely properly sober.

I fancy he used to reason that drink helped his rhetoric. In point of fact, he rarely opened his mouth without making an ass of himself.

With Bolshevik troops to the east of Askhabad and at Astrakhan, the Turks installed at Baku and Jones and his men isolated from support in the direction of Persia, food and fuel shortages became acute. This in turn affected the operating of the railways, and shortages of money soon also threatened the line with paralysis as workers threatened to strike. Besides routine matters of administration which directly bore on British interests, such as the establishing of a hospital for her sick and wounded, Jones was increasingly drawn into the resolution of political disputes between contending parties, to the extent that he at times felt the whole burden of the state shifting to him. This was exacerbated by his command of Russian, unique among Britishers in Askhabad. Britain was now steadily increasing her hold on the Caspian, and this had caused some concern among Russian troops. However, the possibility of Krasnovodsk falling to the enemy – notwithstanding the presence there of a British garrison – could not be dismissed. The whole situation and Britain's involvement was complicated by a developing refugee problem caused by the advance on Baku of Turkish forces and ongoing military action against them by various forces. It was complicated for Jones personally by the need for tact and diplomacy when attempting to explain British policy across the Caucasus, northern Persia and Transcaspia.

These skills became even more vital because of disagreements and a lack of cooperation between the various British military and naval forces operating there and growing differences between the Turkmen population of Transcaspia and the new regime there. His tact and administrative skills were also crucial when dealing with the increasingly perilous financial situation. Jones was highly critical of the fact that, whilst Britain had entered into a reciprocal assistance agreement with the Transcaspian authorities, she had neither made plain her intentions in the region nor met repeated and urgent requests for money. The 'palliative', when it came – in the form of promissory notes issued and personally signed by Jones and his deputies – was too little, too late.

By New Year's Eve 1918, the situation in Askhabad was on a knife-edge. For some time, Bolshevik agitators had been stoking resentment against the British and at a meeting organised by the agitators on 31 December, also attended by Jones's agents, it became apparent that even the loyalties of Funtikov and his fellow politicians could not be counted upon. This, and threats of violent action by Bolsheviks prompted immediate action from Jones. Warning notices were passed in the meeting and it was announced that the building was surrounded. With some relief on Jones's part, the meeting broke up.

Jones's position became daily more exasperating. The newly formed Committee of Public Safety appeared to have attracted some popular support but Malleson, and other more distant 'generals in brass hats and politicians in frock coats', refused to finance it. Jones was left carrying the can; trying, on the one hand, to prevent the railwaymen from attacking the committee and, on the other, continuing to round up Bolshevik agitators. As he recalled, 'I was disgusted with the constant necessity of lying and prevaricating day after day. I was in fact sick and weary of the whole thing and instead of being proud of my position as Representative of Great Britain, I was heartily ashamed of the ignominious rôle I was continuously called upon to play.' More positively, Jones's position did enable him to meet many exotically attired Turkmen chieftains, one of whom, Haji Murat, a Russian-speaker, made a great impression on him.

His position also provided opportunity for more clandestine activities, to which Jones could not officially admit. On several occasions, Haji Murat had requested his company on adventures beyond Askhabad – although it was officially understood that Jones never left the city. Jones recalled: 'Unofficially, many things are possible. I fear that my old Peshawar habits of sneaking into *caravanserai*, hobnobbing with camel-men and generally venturing where self-respecting angels would fear to tread, would now and then prove too strong for me.' Jones also found relief in night-time forays in search of Bolshevik agitators with Drushkin, the sinister Astrakhani Jew and head of CID: 'I was always very careful. If Drushkin suggested that he had a particularly interesting "crib to crack", or as he would call it, a "liquidation to carry out", and I might like to go along, one could be quite certain that one would be kept well out of harm's way. . . . No British officer, let alone the British Representative, would have been seen on such occasions – merely an extra member of Drushkin's militia bodyguard.' Yet, for all these escapades, Jones realised that the stand-off between the Askhabad and Soviet forces could not last and that, sooner or later, Britain would withdraw. When, in January 1919, Jones and his men left Askhabad, it was with 'mixed feelings of relief and sadness'. Though full of hope and romantic ideas on his arrival, the 'Trans-Caspian dream . . . was ending in tragedy'.

* * *

Whatever Malleson thought of Jones's activities – apparently, he never even thanked him – Jarvis thought highly of Jones and his achievements. In February 1919, he recommended him strongly to the War Office for further employment in the Caucasus or the Middle East. As Jarvis noted, he had served with Jones for seven months in conditions of extreme difficulty. Their line of command to India had, as Jarvis recalled, been no less than ten thousand miles and for the duration of that period, Jones had been the 'symbol of British prestige and authority in Transcaspia'. He continued: 'If you have any assignment in connection with Russia, the Caucasus, or Asia Minor, whatever the work is and one man can do it . . .'. The result of this and other efforts to find further employment, led not surprisingly to the doors of SIS. That organisation, which had almost certainly got wind of Jones's activities, contacted their man in Constantinople, Major Vivian, who, besides taking Jones under his wing, was also allegedly responsible some years later for recruiting Kim Philby.

Jarvis's recommendation was, in fact, the first indication that we have of Jones having changed his name to Ronald Sinclair, the name by which he was apparently known for the remainder of his life and which will be used hereafter. Peter Hopkirk, in his edition of Sinclair's diaries, from which some of this story is told, has explained in some detail the nature of Jones/Sinclair's involvement in the execution of twenty-six Bolshevik commissars who were despatched from Baku when its fall to Turkish troops seemed imminent. That incident, though important, is not the focus of this chapter. Rather, we will now turn to the remainder of Sinclair's remarkable life, some of which can be pieced together from scattered files among several archives.

On his return to London from Askhabad, Sinclair divided his time between the War, Foreign and India Offices and apparently established close links with sections of military intelligence. There then followed, over two years, what he described as a 'roving assignment as political observer and liaison officer between the High Commissioner . . . and our naval and military forces in the area of the Black Sea'. In part, this rôle consisted of compiling detailed reports on the region. Some of these were situation reports, describing the dispositions of Soviet troops in the Caucasus and beyond. Others focused on the politics and economics of particular groups or nations, or on the policies of France and Turkey in the region. Yet their purpose – to monitor Soviet activities – was unmistakable; as was, indeed, Sinclair's view as to what policy Britain should adopt. As he noted: 'The issues appear quite clear – a general flare-up and anarchy throughout the Caucasus – or prompt and effective intervention by the Allies.' Though some senior political and military figures agreed, financial and political considerations pushed British policy in exactly the opposite direction. Increasingly, Sinclair's work and that of other British personnel in the region became a holding operation, an attempt to bolster native opposition to the

Bolsheviks. From Constantinople, which was occupied by British, French and Italian contingents, Sinclair liaised with the forces and senior officers of anti-Bolshevik groups, principally those of General Wrangel. Wrangel, for whom Sinclair evidently had some respect, did not, however, gain the unequivocal support of the British Cabinet and his forces eventually succumbed to the Bolshevik advance. Yet Britain was not the only country to have despatched an intelligence officer to the region. Attached to an American Naval Intelligence Mission to southern Russia in 1920, was a dashing young naval officer, Hugo Koehler. Koehler, an ardent and well-connected Anglophile and an accomplished linguist, went in the capacity of a special agent, though was frequently disguised as a peasant.

By the autumn of 1920, the situation in the Crimea was critical. At a secret meeting with General Wrangel on board ship at Sevastopol, Sinclair learned that a Bolshevik onslaught was now almost inevitable. Wrangel feared that this would create a serious refugee problem, with thousands of displaced families converging on Constantinople. Having reported this to General Harrington in Constantinople on the following day, Sinclair was immediately placed in charge of the refugee situation. On his arrival he had been requested by the Foreign Office and by prominent individuals to try and rescue British subjects who had been imprisoned in Baku by the Bolsheviks. Admittedly, these duties were interspersed with more lighthearted moments. When travelling through the Caucasus, one evening Sinclair accompanied Colonel Stokes, on special duties with the Georgian Republic, to the Georgian national opera in Batum. In the course of the performance, Sinclair realised that he was being 'subjected to a close and continuous scrutiny' by two 'very unprepossessing' Jewish ladies, who had yet to be trained in the finer aspects of covert surveillance by their Bolshevik masters.

His rôle as liaison officer called for diplomacy, a quick brain and an equally strong head. As one of the few British officers fluent in Russian, he was expected to appear at every official social occasion where toasts drunk with the locally brewed beverage were frequent and obligatory. There was also much travel around the Caucasus and along the Anatolian coasts, 'showing the flag'. As Sinclair knew only too well, this was a rearguard action. This was clearly demonstrated when, having just toasted the official birth of the Georgian state and its government, Sinclair decided to re-acquaint himself with Batum and to clear his head with a walk in the snow. Walking in the direction of a favourite shop to buy some bottles of wine, Sinclair was almost knocked over by its owner. The shopkeeper, who had already evacuated his family, was all for continuing to the port and the final steamer out of the city, only being persuaded to return to his shop in great haste by the sight of a five pound note. The shopkeeper feared the arrival of hundreds of Soviet soldiers, who would undoubtedly ransack every shop in sight in search of alcohol. Typically enigmatic, Sinclair noted in his diary that he got his wine and the shopkeeper got his five pound note – for which he was prepared to swap his entire stock. What exactly happened on that occasion, Sinclair noted, was 'too fantastic' to record in his diary and belonged elsewhere so we shall never know. Though he and the shopkeeper each got what they wanted, 'that [was] very far from being the whole story'.

The next two decades of Sinclair's career remain something of a mystery. His alleged involvement in the massacre of the Bolshevik commissars made it imperative for him to keep a low profile and it seems likely that he, or his superiors, actually feared for his safety. Apparently for that reason he had changed his name. As Peter Hopkirk has noted, this was done without any publicity. There is, indeed, no evidence among surviving records at the PRO that it was done officially by deed poll and as Hopkirk has further suggested, the India Office was clearly anxious not to advertise it in any other way. Why he was referred to by his alias in February 1919 is difficult to say. It is possible that he may have used this name before when on intelligence duties or that, if SIS hoped to deploy him anywhere on the borders of the Russian Empire, it would be better if his real identity were not known. Of course it is also possible that Sinclair anticipated criticism concerning the incident and took steps to protect himself. What we do know is that both names continued to be used in official contexts over the next few years. In 1922, Sinclair was detained in London to help the Foreign Office compile a response to further Soviet charges made against him in connection with the Baku commissars. Intriguingly, in surviving Foreign Office files from that episode, he twice signed himself Teague-Jones, 'Indian Police'. Elsewhere, however, in a report of the Interdepartmental Committee on Eastern Unrest, he was referred to as Major Teague-Jones, 'late of the SIS', and was thanked by the committee for his work on its behalf. A new position with the Indian Police would certainly have made sense.

Clearly, Sinclair was a highly skilled intelligence agent but he needed to find a new career that would avoid the attentions of his Soviet detractors. A position with the Indian Police would also tie in, to some extent, with the fact that some years later, in the early 1930s, he was obviously still resident in India but entitled to 'leave', which, sometimes alone and sometimes with a fellow officer, he spent travelling widely throughout Asia, Africa and Europe, generally by car. This led to an extensive body of articles written for various newspapers and journals, including the *Morris*, the *Times of India Annual*, the *Journal of the Royal Central Asian Society*, *Review of India*, and the *Field*. Sinclair's travels were also reported in *The Times* and in the *Tatler*. From the latter we know that, in February 1928, whilst reputedly 'on leave', Sinclair traversed India from Bombay, then travelled by car to the North-West Frontier and Khyber Pass, and back through Persia and the Middle East, reaching England in early May. He then continued to France, Switzerland and the Pyrenees and back to London. His car, a Morris Oxford that he named Bigly, after the Urdu for 'lightning', was then shipped back to India where he continued from Madras through southern India, north to Delhi and back to Bombay – a total distance of some

20,000 miles without mechanical failure. In the following year, accompanied by two other Englishmen, Sinclair was motoring in Ceylon (Sri Lanka) and narrowly missed death when his car was struck by lightning. Again, in 1929 Sinclair crossed Southern India to Bombay, caught a steamer to East Africa, and motored through Kenya and Uganda to the source of the Nile. After visiting the Sudan he went north to Egypt and the Mediterranean. His surviving travel writings suggest that he also visited Burma, Bahrein, Malta and Abyssinia, although he travelled most extensively in the Middle East.

Quite what purpose this travelling had is unclear. Sinclair was a man of great curiosity and had wide-ranging interests which, among other things, encompassed art, archaeology and the paranormal. However, besides indulging these and other tastes, an official or semi-official brief also seems possible. Early in 1932 Sinclair received a letter from Hugh MacGregor, Information Officer at the India Office, in which the latter thanked him for a report that had clearly provided either political or economic information. In this letter MacGregor suggested that it would be useful if Sinclair would continue to supply such information from time to time.

More concrete evidence of an official connection might be detected more clearly in the mid-1920s. In 1926, Sinclair had journeyed alone by car from Beirut to Bombay, the first time that this had been accomplished. In the published version of this account, *Adventures in Persia: To India by the Back Door*, Sinclair noted in the introduction that the journey was undertaken in response to a request received by the Board of Trade from a group of wealthy northern English manufacturers to discover trading conditions in Persia. According to his own testimony, a Jim Bradley of the Board of Trade recommended Sinclair to them. I have been unable to trace an employee of this name at the Board of Trade among surviving records of that department at the PRO and Peter Hopkirk has suggested that Sinclair's journey may have been a cover for intelligence-gathering activities. Yet the two were not mutually exclusive. Sidney Reilly and the British agent, Captain George Hill, known as 'IK8', were apparently infiltrated into southern Russia late in 1918 with credentials provided by the Department of Overseas Trade. As far as Sinclair was concerned, it seems that his employment with the Indian Police may have been interrupted or ended prior to 1926.

The importance of commercial intelligence in the official mind had been increasing since the establishment in 1899 of the Commercial Intelligence section of the Board of Trade. That section had grown significantly during the First World War and, in 1927, Britain was in any case to sign a trade agreement with Persia. It would therefore be vital for private interests and departments in Whitehall to have accurate intelligence about commercial and other conditions in the country. Prior to his departure, when lunching with the head of the Imperial Bank of Persia, Sinclair was told that branches of the bank and British Consulates would assist his passage through Persia. Board of Trade confidential reports held at the PRO (under reference BT 196) suggest that the board regularly fielded such enquiries from private concerns and that some of these enquiries related to Persia. Early in 1927, a report noted that the department had given assistance to a Mr M.H. Ellis, who was travelling by car on behalf of firms in the motor trade through Europe, Asia, and India en route for Australia. It is also possible that, by the early 1930s, perhaps as a result of his highly successful mission on behalf of the Board of Trade, Sinclair was being used in connection with the Trade Commissioners' service. Several middle-ranking military officers occupied posts of this kind in the Dominions and, whilst Sinclair's name has not appeared in the relatively few records relating to these positions, from a later newspaper clipping among his papers, we do know that Sinclair 'conducted trade surveys throughout Asia' for ten years after the First and Second World Wars. At any rate, Sinclair's journey from Beirut to Baghdad and across Persia provided additional opportunities for adventure which deserve further mention.

Having bought himself a shiny, black, model A-Ford – Zobeida, as he christened it – Sinclair lost no time in making contact with those in Beirut who were able to provide him with valuable information not only about motoring conditions, but also with valuable political information. Having set off as part of a large convoy of vehicles across the Syrian Desert, on reaching Palmyra Sinclair discovered that two Arabs whom he had grudgingly consented to carry as passengers, were in fact wanted by the police and had been arrested overnight. At this stage, Sinclair's attention was focused on the history and beauty of the Arab Middle East. His mind, ever storing information both for official purposes and for his feature writing, conjured with ancient historical scenes, and with the culture, art and society of the region. Having left Palmyra, Sinclair encountered his first dust storm, a 'black impenetrable cloud' in which he and the driver of the vehicle ahead, which he was closely following, could see nothing and soon lost their way. Finally reaching Baghdad, Sinclair found a room booked for him at the Maude hotel. There, besides exotic scenes and a degree of comfort, he found a 'chipped enamel wash basin, a soap-dish with a thin tablet of bright pink highly scented soap, evidently left by the last occupant, a galvanised iron hip-bath, and the inevitable wooden thunder-box'. As he continued, 'Its lid was open to show that it was empty and ready for service, and on the upper edge of the lid where it rested against the wall, a large scorpion was airing itself.'

However, the hotel at least provided a base from which he could interview applicants for the position of guide for the next leg of his journey into Persia. That section of his journey would take him through highly dangerous territory. The route was perilous and the driving conditions difficult and, after some unsuitable applicants, one Abdul Samad, a native of Isfahan, was duly appointed. Although his mechanical and driving skills proved non-existent, Abdul at least provided interesting conversation and, for the next part of the journey, two militiamen foisted upon Sinclair by an anxious border guard provided some protection from the bandits that inhabited the region.

Having reached Hamadan, Sinclair recorded the hospitality of the local manager of the Imperial Bank of Persia. There, Sinclair gleaned valuable information about local trading conditions from the manager and from leading merchants and notables. He also observed other traffic on the road, noting the covered wagons or *fourgons*, on which the drivers lay covered by and often asleep in their Persian carpets, and which, to Sinclair's keen eye, often carried Russian imports. However, there was also evidence of British and Indian goods bound for distant parts of Persia on camel or donkey. At Tabriz, where Sinclair stayed with the British Consul, he met several government officials as well as merchants and apparently obtained more useful information.

There was also the exotic in abundance. At Qazvin, Sinclair, having enquired about a hotel room was asked if he would share a room. There he encountered the 'biggest and most picturesque specimen of a Kurd I had ever seen outside of a picture book'. Besides his silver-hilted dagger and headdress, there was a large water-pipe, from which he inhaled 'great mouthfuls of smoke, drawing it deep down into his lungs, and then exhaling it in long streamers which curled up towards the solitary electric light bulb . . .'.

Besides the risk of bandits, there were other dangers closer to hand. Zobeida, being light and therefore easily lifted from a ditch, was well fitted to the journey but the water-channels or *joobs* which punctuated the highway, could be several feet deep and wide, and appeared suddenly and without warning, threatened to break the chassis. Usually these were best dealt with by a quick burst of speed; but, in other sections of the journey, Sinclair was forced to rebuild parts of the road and even to push the overheating car before he could proceed. Approaching the Manjil Pass beyond Tabriz, Sinclair found himself on what had suddenly become a narrow, grass-bordered lane, several inches deep in mud. Without warning, a caravan of Russian wagons appeared, travelling at high speed. Sinclair swerved onto the verge. Under its weight the verge gave way and Zobeida slid towards the abyss.

Sinclair and Abdul managed to scramble clear as the car clung to the rock face by a single wheel. Having rescued Zobeida with the help of some local villagers, as night descended rapidly, the car's headlights failed. Conditions became dangerous and Sinclair was aware that the Vice-Consul at Resht was expecting him and had strongly advised him to arrive before nightfall. Having again narrowly missed disaster, on this occasion in the shape of a convoy of speeding cars that Sinclair suspected of being the Soviet Trade Delegation bound for Tehran, he finally reached Resht, 'to find an anxious Vice-Consul awaiting me with drinks, a hot bath and an appetising dinner'. On the following day he visited the Caspian and, to the visible annoyance of some of its crew, photographed a Soviet naval gunboat.

In Tehran, Sinclair stayed ten days with the British Commercial Attaché and besides picnicking, historical excursions and enjoying the generosity of his host, Sinclair returned to his former habits of prowling in the 'semi-darkness of the bazaars'. In pursuit of commercial intelligence, he spent a good deal of time in discussion with local tradesmen, consuming vast quantities of hot, sweet tea to 'an accompaniment of grumbling camels, cursing mule-drivers, and the soporific bubbling of water-pipes'. As he continued, the mass of information thus accumulated was later condensed into reports 'for my London friends'. From Tehran, Sinclair passed to Qum and thence to the beautiful city of Isfahan where he stayed with a bank manager, who was able to provide introductions to local merchants. Although Sinclair found the wealthier classes less forthcoming, he obtained much valuable information from others, which he wrote up in the evenings. This, as he recorded, left him time to explore the cities along his route. He was also greatly aided by the presence of Abdul, whose forthright manner and sensitivity to local custom and manners was indispensable. This was demonstrated when dealing with the owner of a donkey that Sinclair had run over when his brakes failed and which, to the astonishment of everyone, appeared unharmed when disentangled from the undercarriage of his car. So it was with some surprise that Sinclair found himself advised sternly by Abdul not to proceed beyond Shiraz. Further, Abdul, who was recovering from malaria, stated that anyone who agreed to accompany Sinclair must either be 'mentally afflicted or a scoundrel, and would assuredly let [him] down, if he did not actually cut [his] throat.' Whatever else, as Consul Chick warned him in parting, Sinclair must at all costs avoid Niriz, a haven for bandits and a place where Sinclair would certainly meet with an unpleasant end.

As Sinclair recorded, his problems began almost immediately. First, there was Hassan, Abdul's replacement. Surly and unsmiling, he was also forgetful: having failed to pack a can of oil that was urgently required when Zobeida's engine overheated, the car had to make do instead with mustard oil, which Sinclair obtained during a nerve-racking visit to Niriz. Then, in the gathering darkness and in complete wilderness, the headlights failed. Hassan, terrified by a night in the open, left Sinclair, armed with a can of corned beef and a shotgun, to the local banditry. It was, in fact, only his experience that saved him on this occasion. From behind a protective wall, Sinclair spotted a group of moving shadows. Realising that he must improvise or die, he laughed loudly and began to converse with imaginary companions. This was enough to scare the group away but he was obliged to remain awake for the remainder of the night. On the following day, the road continued to climb steeply. Zobeida's wheels frequently teetered on the verge of a drop of several hundred feet, the road appearing high above him in a sweeping curve as he turned each corner. Finally, the car stalled and stopped dead. Just ahead was a section of the road that had partly collapsed and was blocked by a large boulder. With his car jack and working with great perseverance in the blistering heat, Sinclair eventually tipped the great boulder into the ravine below. He then set about repairing the road and again unloaded Zobeida, whose engine had now cooled. The engine started again and Sinclair, at times running uphill beside the car with only inches between him and a sheer drop, managed to proceed. With some despair Sinclair, having at last reached the top, now contemplated returning on foot some considerable distance to collect all the paraphernalia of his journey, including even the back seat of the car, fuel and food which he had offloaded to lighten the vehicle.

After a brief halt in Kirman, Sinclair again demonstrated his lust for adventure. A telegram arrived from the 'board of directors' for whom he was gathering information, instructing him to head immediately for India to investigate there and in countries further to the east, their existing organisation. Rather than head for Baghdad, Basra and a steamer to Bombay, he opted – against all advice – for an extremely difficult route directly eastwards. As he recalled, he had some years earlier travelled from Baluchistan to Khorasan and was aware of what awaited him: '. . . apart from anything else there was a challenge about the venture which appealed to me – I just could not bring myself to turn back, with this tract of unknown country luring me on'. Whilst preparing for this final leg of his journey, Sinclair visited the old fortress of Bam. There, as he wandered among the extensive ruins, he detected a movement and, hearing some startled ravens overhead, decided to investigate. Just then a large piece of coping from the building came crashing down behind him. Further dangers awaited Sinclair as he left Kirman. It soon became clear that the desert contained large patches of quicksand and Zobeida, her radiator boiling continuously in the intense heat, became stuck repeatedly, finally stalling and refusing to restart or dislodge itself from the sand. Nursing a terrible headache and sucking a pebble to maintain a flow of saliva, Sinclair tried every conceivable solution to move the car and it was only when a tyre burst spontaneously as he dozed that he had the idea of deflating all of the tyres in order to move more effectively across the sand. To the heat and sand were added further landslides, severe thunderstorms and a very large, dead and rapidly decomposing camel, which Sinclair had also to negotiate and which had been abandoned where it had dropped, in a narrow canyon. At last, however, Sinclair limped towards Duzdap and a stunned Welsh superintendent of the Indo-European Telegraph Company. Although frustrated when told that he could not continue by car due to the state of the roads, Sinclair was heartened by the news that he was the first motorist ever to have made the last section of the journey from Kirman alone – 'honour was satisfied'.

*   *   *

From surviving details among his papers it is possible tentatively to reconstruct Sinclair's subsequent career. It seems possible that he remained in the employment of the Board of Trade or the Indian Police or both until the first years of the Second World War. At that stage the evidence again becomes confusing. As Hopkirk has noted, an envelope among Sinclair's papers at the Imperial War Museum which bears the title 'Maj. Sinclair, MI5 War Office' and which apparently dates from 1940, suggests that on the outbreak of war, if not earlier, Sinclair was recruited by the Security Service. Rather more revealing is a memorandum on Bermuda and its security by Sinclair dating from June 1941. As part of the 'lend-lease' agreement, the United States had given Britain fifty destroyers in exchange for British bases in the Caribbean, Bermuda and Newfoundland. Searches among relevant papers at the PRO imply that Sinclair was sent to Bermuda as a result of an enquiry generated by the Colonial Office in December 1940. It seems that a vital naval base in Bermuda, which provided cover for Atlantic convoys, lacked any security protection. Although thousands of tourists flocked annually to Bermuda, visas were not required and arrangements for obtaining an American passport were extremely lax. The island achieved greater importance by virtue of the arrival of a detachment of the Imperial Censorship department, whose task was to examine all correspondence going between Europe and the Americas.

During a week's on-the-spot survey of the problem, Sinclair interviewed senior British and American personnel, including the British governor, and several prominent civilians. His conclusion, that the perspective of governor Knollys and his staff was much too parochial, rather confirmed existing fears in London. The focus of his enquiry – Imperial security, local colonial security and the broader context of Anglo-American relations – does suggest a connection with MI5. The nature of the work undertaken by the handful of Security Service officers permanently stationed overseas, the Defence Security Officers (DSOs) as they were known, ties in closely with Sinclair's concerns at this time. Yet his name is not among a list of pre-war Security Service personnel working overseas, now publicly available. Nor does his name appear in a similar list for the war itself. However, that list does not include the United States and, by Sinclair's own account, from 1941 he lived in New York.

The precise nature of his position may never be entirely clear but available evidence points to employment in the early stages of the war by MI5 under the aegis of British Security Coordination (BSC) which came into being early in 1941 under Sir William Stephenson. That organisation was based in New York and provided a channel for the activities and interests of the Security Service, SIS, and other security and intelligence bodies throughout the Americas. More fundamentally, it was initiated to protect extensive British interests in the United States which were vital to the war effort and which, until the signing of the lend-lease agreements in the spring of 1941, were not formally protected in any way by the United States authorities. The ten million or so German- or Italian-speaking Americans had to be watched – especially where their work brought them into contact with goods bound for Britain. This was also true of the extensive network of German agents in the country and the many other groups of nationalist Indians, left-wing propagandists and Fenians. It seems likely that Sinclair was brought in to assist the activities of the Security Division of BSC under Sir Conop

Guthrie. Besides a broad range of counter-subversive activities aimed at protecting British shipping and property, BSC also spread pro-British propaganda and, in terms of activities beyond the United States, trained American and Canadian agents for parachute landings in occupied Europe and penetrated Japanese, Spanish, Italian and Vichy French diplomacy.

Sinclair's involvement with BSC is hinted at by his activity in Bermuda, where the DSOs had close contact with BSC in New York. From surviving evidence it seems that, for several years, Sinclair was part of this evolving relationship across Bermuda and the Caribbean. In July 1944 he was appointed as a consul at the Consulate General in New York. Though he features in this capacity in the printed *Foreign Office List*, I have found no mention of him among surviving files of the Consulate General itself. Admittedly, many were deliberately destroyed after the war but from other sources it seems very likely that he continued to work for BSC on a broad range of intelligence matters. These included Bermuda and the Caribbean but, more significantly, he also now gathered material on Indian movements in the United States and this was channelled to the Director of Intelligence Bureau, Delhi, via the British Embassy in Washington and the India Office. From a surviving letter of thanks from the India Office shortly before its dissolution in 1947, we know that Sinclair had built up a broad network of sources for this intelligence and that, with Independence, his 'special appointment' was due to end. It seems that Sinclair then, oddly perhaps, offered his services both to the Pakistani Ambassador and to a former contact at the India Office, P.J. Patrick, in connection with negotiations between India and Pakistan over Kashmir. The nature of Sinclair's involvement in these talks is unclear except to say that he was congratulated on their conclusion by Patrick, then attached to the British delegation to the United Nations.

Shortly afterwards, Sinclair was promoted to head the Commercial Department of the New York Consulate General.

This probably brought him into contact again with his old colleagues, in the form of the Commercial Relations and Export Department of the Board of Trade. The records of this secretive department do not survive in quantity but it is clear that it liaised closely with the Foreign Office. Like British Security Coordination, it was responsible for promoting and securing British commercial interests in the United States and Sinclair was clearly successful in this work. He was also much in demand around this time as an after-dinner speaker, a platform that evidently provided him with opportunities for propagandising on Britain's behalf.

Sinclair's wartime involvement with BSC is also strongly hinted at by other documents among his papers. Firstly, there is correspondence with Charles 'Dick' Ellis, author of *The Transcaspian Episode* (1963). Ellis had himself served briefly in the region during the First World War before joining SIS in 1923. By that time, of course, Sinclair had left, possibly for the Indian Police. A social relationship is also possible, as both men were apparently members of the Travellers' Club. More likely still is that the two men worked together in America when Ellis was Sir William Stephenson's deputy at BSC. This is also suggested by a letter from 1962 among papers at the India Office Library, in which Ellis noted that Stephenson wished him to go to New York in connection with the publication of H. Montgomery Hyde's biography of Stephenson. Notably, Hyde was himself from 1939 an SIS officer employed by BSC and was also its official historian. In fact, late in 1940, he had been attached to the Imperial Censorship office in Bermuda by SIS and, in that position, was instrumental in penetrating a network of German agents which, when it was traced, led straight to the head of the Gestapo, Heinrich Himmler. His dates of service with BSC were almost exactly the same as those of Sinclair. Hyde was also later called to refute charges levelled against Sinclair in a Soviet account of the massacre of the twenty-six commissars and also reviewed Ellis's book.

The Security Service has now released substantial quantities of records but, whilst useful, these are carefully selected and generally reveal only part of the picture – usually a partial outline or some information on particular cases in which that organisation was involved. Of Sinclair, I have found no trace. Peter Hopkirk has mentioned, in connection with the Baku commissar incident especially, Sinclair's effort to retain anonymity in later life and his eventual move from New York to Spain. There, it seems, besides corresponding with former colleagues from his days in intelligence work, he also maintained a keen interest in world affairs and, in particular, events in the Middle East, Central Asia and Russia. His papers contain many extensive typewritten summaries of historical events and political developments either compiled by him or taken from published works, as if he intended to produce a lengthy historical work. Perhaps this material formed the basis for after-dinner speeches or was simply a means of sharpening his intellect. Besides this work, it seems that Sinclair also travelled quite often and possibly worked in a minor rôle for the Foreign Office, reporting on British commercial activities overseas into the early 1960s. However, owing to his natural discretion, as much as to the sensitive nature of the material itself (if it survives), the full story of Sinclair's eventful and dangerous life is unlikely ever to be known.

Butterfly hunting in Dalmatia (spy pretends to hunt butterflies)

2

The Case of 'The Queer Accountant'

FROM CONSTANTINOPLE TO BEIRUT

In the early summer of 1917, Special Agent Clifford G. Beckham gained entry to a small cottage near Bay, St Louis. A rapid search of the premises confirmed his worst fears, that it was a nest of German agents. The occupants of the house, a Mr and Mrs Ely Soane, had been under observation for some time. Rumours that Ely Soane, a British subject, had been meeting regularly with German suspects, had reached the British Consul at New Orleans, and he had persuaded the Department of Justice to act.

Soane, it seems, met frequently with the wife of a German, Otto Lehmann, president of a trading company with key interests in Nicaragua. Further investigations of Lehmann's background linked him to activities aimed at promoting the German commercial submarine service in America. Lehmann's associates included one Wettstein, whom Clifford Beckham considered a 'German of the officer type and probably a very dangerous man'. These connections, and letters in German found by Beckham linking Soane to a pro-German and 'notorious' newspaper, caused some concern. Added to this, Soane's wife was believed to be German. Soane himself, a British Vice-Consul in Persia, had interests in the oil industry and had also apparently recently applied for American citizenship.

Investigations within the Foreign Office suggested that E.B. Soane was a man of 'great linguistic and other attainments', that he had been particularly well thought of in 1911, in spite of an unspecified 'moral lapse' in 1908 which he had apparently 'lived down'. Further enquiries with the India Office and with the British authorities in Persia lent an even stranger twist to the tale. For it seems that Soane had been an assistant political officer under Sir Percy Cox, Chief Political Officer of the British force in Mesopotamia, since January 1916 and could not therefore have been in St Louis when his wife claimed he had been. Some Foreign Office officials even doubted that Soane was married at all.

These and other doubts afflicted Mr J. Carlisle, the British Consul at New Orleans, when in May 1917 he unexpectedly had an interview with Mrs Soane, who had come to the Consulate to renew her passport. At that meeting, Carlisle convinced himself that she was who she claimed to be. However, from other evidence it was quite impossible that Ely Soane had recently been in America. Carlisle had stumbled on the truth – Soane was being impersonated.

Soane's wife had moved to the United States in the autumn of 1914, apparently to avoid suspicion and persecution as an alien resident in England. At this stage, Soane had been a prisoner of the Turks in Baghdad. Ely Soane later applied for American citizenship on his wife's behalf but was prevented by official duty from regular personal contact with her. He was, therefore, quite unaware that she had resumed a pre-marital liaison with one John Nesere, a former journalist whom she had met some years earlier in Ostend. Nesere, as a suspected German spy, and on account of his impersonation, languished in a federal prison for a year whilst Mrs Soane, an astoundingly duplicitous woman, left for Atlanta, never to be heard of again. As far as the British government was concerned, one official observed, the issue now had two aspects, one of which Soane might wish to deal with in the divorce courts; the other – 'the impersonation of a British official' – would be left to the Foreign Office and to Mr Carlisle.

This unusual episode was typical of the remarkable life of a remarkable man: Ely Bannister Soane, banker, linguist, writer, soldier, engineer, intelligence agent and British Consul. Soane was undoubtedly brilliant. Small and stocky in build, dark haired and with 'keen, piercing eyes', he had a forceful personality and was utterly fearless. When, towards the end of his life, Soane undertook political duties in Persia and Kurdistan, his exceptional abilities with tribes afforded him an almost mythical status in their eyes and among colleagues. Yet, in keeping with the peculiarities of Soane's life, some years earlier several senior figures in government had tried to have him legally prevented from re-entering Persia.

By 1912, the Imperial Bank of Persia had branches throughout the spheres of interest and neutrality created by the Anglo-Russian Convention of 1907. For the young and adventurous, the bank offered a route to the Orient and a less conventional life. An accomplished linguist and thespian but shy as a schoolboy, Soane apparently drifted into banking and three and half years' service with Messrs H.S. King and Co., 'East India Bankers & Agents'. In 1902 he was recruited by the Imperial Bank and over the next five years contributed to the expansion of its activities, with postings in Tehran, Yazd, Bushire, Shiraz and finally in Karmansha, where he became branch manager. Then, suddenly, in 1907 Soane resigned.

In a tribute to Soane, Sir Percy Cox's successor as (Acting) Civil Commissioner in Baghdad, Arnold Talbot Wilson, noted that Soane, within a year of starting to learn Persian, had begun a translation of Omar Khayyam. By 1904–5, Soane was in Shiraz, where, driven by an insatiable curiosity, he had taken to disguising himself as a Persian and, in the darkness of night, mixing with Shirazi mullahs. Within a year, he had converted to Islam. Though an astute businessman, Soane was too quixotic for banking. His intellectual passions and his fierce and wayward nature drew him to a more dangerous life. Formerly suited, moustached and dapper, if never quite respectable, in 1907 Ghulam Husain, aka Ely Bannister Soane, commenced two years of wandering in native disguise from Constantinople to Beirut, and thence to the mountainous areas of Kurdistan.

Intertwined with Soane's exceptional abilities, courage and adventurous spirit, was an equally beguiling aberrant streak, occasionally revealed in unpleasant episodes, in his correspondence and in tussles with superiors. Arnold Wilson claimed that, in 1907, Soane had resigned willingly as a result of a dispute with the Russian Consul at Shiraz. Sir Thomas Jackson, Managing Director of the Imperial Bank, declared that Soane had left in bad health on a medical certificate and that he had gone on leave. Yet the files of the Foreign and India Offices are more fulsome.

Soane's promotion to manager had not met with universal praise. The bank's chief manager in Persia had objected on the grounds that it would displease the British Legation. According to him, Soane had been expelled from Persia in 1906. The board of the Imperial Bank knew nothing of this but was aware that, when at Bushire and Shiraz, Soane's 'friendship and correspondence with foreigners excited criticism and complaint'. However, this had apparently been satisfactorily explained and Soane's conduct since had been exemplary. Further investigations within the Foreign Office and at the British Embassy in Tehran revealed that Soane had 'acted as an informal agent to the Russian Consul-General', and had refused to be registered as a British subject. When the issue was forced, Soane became obstinate to the point where his expulsion was being discussed. Over a year later, in November 1908, Sir George Barclay, the newly appointed British Ambassador in Tehran, requested that Soane be legally prevented from re-entering the country. According to his information, Soane had probably left the bank due to his 'irregular conduct, especially with regard to women'. Barclay had acted on a 'very serious complaint' made against Soane, who had allegedly abducted a married woman and taken her to Baghdad. Though convinced that the woman in question was a 'bad lot', it was felt that Soane had compromised himself and that, if he were to return to Persia, he might 'excite a breach of the peace'. Debate raged within the Foreign Office, in Tehran, at the Imperial Bank, and at the British Museum which, briefly, was held to have sponsored Soane's wanderings in Kurdistan. Soane, in the words of one official, was 'so infernally crooked' and such a 'pestilential fellow' that he must resign. In short, he was a 'liar' and there was 'no place in Persia where he would not be a constant source of trouble'.

Could this have been a manufactured cover? Probably not, but whatever the truth of this episode, on his arrival in Constantinople on the first leg of his journey, Soane did not intend to dwell on it. Having returned from a short and comfortable leave in England, Soane wished to ease himself back into the 'magnetism' of the east. Though his detractors believed him to be working on behalf of the British Museum or an Oriental society in England, Soane apparently travelled as a private individual. His stay in Constantinople was designed to afford him a 'delectable resting-place, a point from which to look out upon East and West with equal facility'. Each would contribute the 'features necessary to a pleasant life' – books and libraries on the one hand, and on the other a 'way of escape among oriental people and surroundings, without necessitating a longer journey and a longer bill'.

This combination of curiosity for language and culture, together with an element of escapism, underpinned Soane's decision to travel in disguise. In fact, as Soane recalled, he had little money and the inflated costs of travel as a European were beyond his means. He continued: 'If I went I must don a fez and pass as a native of the East, must buy my own food, and do my own haggling, must do all those things which no European could or would ever think of doing.' If his disguise failed entirely to convince then at worst he would probably be accused of being of Persian origin, but certainly not European. In any case, there was the thrill of solitude, 'knowing practically no Turkish or Arabic' and being keenly aware of Muhammedan pieties, prayers and liturgy. In short, Soane observed, travel in disguise 'was cheap, I should see much of the new country, and many new tribes. I should learn many more

Kurdish dialects, and when I had finished, should be in a possession of a truer knowledge of the people, their ways and nature, than a European possibly could in ten years.'

Despairing of the 'terrible alleys' and ubiquitous 'filth and mire' of Constantinople, Soane was desperately anxious to leave. He found exotic company in a drunken Russian and a Persian sheikh, with whom he conversed and bemoaned the vile weather from beneath a giant, shared quilt. But, as he recalled, he 'yearned for the freedom of plain and mountain, the slow march of the clanging caravan, the droning song of the shepherds on the hills, the fresh open air, and the burning sun'. Having visited Kurdistan in the previous year, Soane was eager to return and waited for a change in the weather to give him his chance.

For all his eccentricity, Soane was in many ways suited to clandestine work. In Constantinople, he had assimilated effortlessly with the French, Armenian, Russian, Balkan and other inhabitants. As he recalled, he quite forgot his intention of learning Turkish, and instead acquired a 'fine proficiency in French' and some Greek. He also ingratiated himself with the Persian Turks of the Great Bazaar, conversing fluently in Persian and passing quite undetected as a native of Shiraz. In fact, so complete was his mastery of disguise and language that when, dressed as a European, he was unexpectedly interviewed by the Persian Consul in Constantinople, the latter refused to believe that he was not a Shirazi and was only convinced on being shown Soane's passport and several letters which proved the point. Similarly, with the Persian Kurds he befriended and with whom he shared tea and cigarettes – besides a hatred of the Turkish weather – Soane found them 'jovial and communicative' and very forthcoming with information about tribes 'that [he] had come to seek, but had not hoped to acquire in the first interview'.

On board the *Saghalien*, bound for Beirut, Soane found himself among quite different people and hearing the first English spoken since his departure for Constantinople. It was at this point that Ely Soane – now disguised by a fez and other eastern clothing – to all intents and purposes disappeared. Besides a party of priests with their charges bound for Jerusalem, there were two large parties of wealthy manufacturers from the Midlands and North of England. There was a smaller group of English clerics, and some Americans, Germans, French and a Turkish family. Feeling 'strangely cut off' from the other Europeans by virtue of his disguise, Soane despised or claimed to despise the religious and social narrow-mindedness of English society. He was contemptuous but mildly envious of their cosseted means of travel, which would in a matter of weeks see them whistled through the Near East in 'special trains and carriages' and 'put up in the best hotels', returning in 'lordly fashion' to England, 'experienced Oriental travellers'. Soane was equally contemptuous of their assumption of racial superiority. He noted:

> It is strange what a simple change of headgear can do. Here was I, by the mere fact of wearing a fez, isolated, looked down upon by types one would pass unnoticed in London, audibly commented upon as 'quite a civilized-looking Turk', exciting wonder as to ''ow many wives 'e's got', and such traditionally Oriental questions. The ignorance of these people was wonderful and colossal.

Yet Soane also enjoyed this episode, the thrill of being taken at face value and being introduced to a third party as if he were a 'rare bug'. As Soane noted, whatever lay in store for these English travellers, he had embarked upon a rather different enterprise, 'to be conducted always with an eye to the elusive piastre, and a ready, lying tongue'.

* * *

En route for Aleppo, on packed and desperately uncomfortable trains, Soane was again surrounded by a welter of races and was duly challenged by a Turkish policeman, obese and squinting in the intense heat, to show his papers. Unable to decide between a

Persian or English identity, Soane feigned complete ignorance, realising that any reasoned attempt to answer the policeman's questions would simply compromise him further. Aleppo, as the first genuinely Arab city on his route, offered sanctuary and it was conveniently located on the road to Kurdistan and Persia. There, besides exploring the older parts of the city, Soane prepared for the remainder of his journey, roaming in the bazaar and building stores of candles, tea, sugar, cheese, fruit and other provisions.

From Aleppo, and the filthy Hotel de Syrie, Soane embarked upon a long ride by traditional Syrian cart through desert and the ancient Hittite settlements to Membich. Munching on dates, onions and flaps of bread, Soane was taken for a *Haji*, returning from the pilgrimage to Mecca. This guaranteed him civil treatment and a degree of safety, so long as he was able to sustain this guise. Although Soane might pretend to despise his fellow European travellers, he was essentially an Englishman accustomed to certain standards. The novelty of having to transport his own luggage and clean for himself came as an unpleasant shock and contrasted with the niceties of eating and greeting and dealing appropriately with eastern peoples, part of the 'generous and genial East' that he loved.

Crossing the Euphrates Valley, Soane's party encountered their first Kurds and Soane, able to speak the language, was treated with some reverence and taken for a fellow Kurd. Soane was captivated by the Kurds – the least-known race of the Middle East, its people spread across 125,000 square miles of Turkey and Persia. Though tarnished by their propensity for feuding and brigandage, Soane considered them the 'bravest, most independent, and intelligent [race] of all'. Through Charmelik, seat of the infamous robber chief Ibrahim Pasha, the caravan began to climb, through gullies and passes and, as Soane recorded, in some discomfort owing to the pitiable state of the roads:

For hours we ascended ravines and slid, banging, down hillsides, boxes and chattels of all descriptions almost taking charge despite their substantial lashings. Do what one might, inconsequent paraphernalia, eatables, small articles, would leap out and roll away, and one had the greatest difficulty in exercising sufficient restraint upon the overwhelming inclination to follow head first. For miles both myself and the driver walked, helping the wheels over rocks, piloting the carriage round the corners of rocky zigzags, or helping the horses in desperate efforts to haul up slopes.

Over equally difficult and dangerous roads the party passed from Urfa to Diarbekir, between the Kawaraja and Kurdish mountain ranges. At Urfa, Soane befriended some Assyrians, having managed to gain their trust as a southern Kurd. With one of them, Soane made frequent excursions to the central bazaar of Urfa accumulating, at no small cost, a quantity of fine Turkish cigarettes. These sustained him through the 'frowning masses of the Kurdish mountains . . . half hidden in black clouds'. As Soane observed, at the highest point of the road, 'one looks down over the undulating desert with a curious feeling of a silent, death-like solitude of infinitely sinister aspect'.

Soane approached Diarbekir with trepidation, fearing that his mode of travel, his conversation with his driver and even his appearance – which all pointed to him being a Muslim – would lead to difficulties if his passport were examined. Should this occur, Soane might be accused of the heinous crime of having stolen it. As he noted, his appearance was extremely damning:

> . . . the weather, too, had done its best to disguise me. I was darkened by wind and sun; nine days' black beard scraped the chest left bare by a buttonless shirt. My trousers were muddy and torn, and I wore a long overcoat, very much like the robes of any of the myriads of Turkish subjects who affect a semi-European dress.

Fortunately for Soane, the passport clerk at the city gates was illiterate and Soane passed into the 'clear, bright, busy city' of

Diarbekir. Soane admired its broad streets, the spring temperatures and the diverse races – Armenians, Kurds, Greeks, Syrians, Chaldeans and Assyrians. There, he was able to study in more detail the characteristics of eastern Christians, whom he generally found wanting in comparison with fellow Muslims.

The opportunity to travel south to Mosul on the Tigris came rather unexpectedly one day as Soane lunched frugally on dry bread and lettuce. Hurriedly, for this was too good a chance to miss, Soane made necessary purchases and presented himself with his new travelling companion, the aged Haji Vali, to the owner of a river craft, a 'cadaverous-looking giant' with a speech impediment and a 'single, fierce-looking eye'. The vessel – a *kalak* – was an oddity: a huge goatskin raft, which could not be propelled but merely shunted towards desired currents, perilously vulnerable to rogue currents and wind. In fine weather it could hardly be a more pleasant mode of travel, revolving slowly in the sunshine, Soane, Haji Vali and the crew brewing tea and enjoying the scenery.

On the third day, amid precipitous mountain scenery, the party faced a powerful gale and for several days their belongings and provisions turned to pulp. Such was Soane's discomfort in a makeshift tent, next to a rheumatic and grizzly Haji Vali, that he spent two nights 'upon the apricots, covered by soaked and clammy things that, whilst they kept the wind off, were so chill as to make their advantage problematical'. In fine weather, on a roaring, flood-swollen river, 'flying along at express speed, and amid cries of "Ya Rebbi! Sahl! Ya Rebbi!"' (Oh God, help! Oh God!) the *kalak* rotated, dodging occasional bullets fired from Kurdish villages on the precipitous slopes. As Soane noted with some incredulity, these and other shooting incidents went practically unnoticed by the crew.

Danger of another kind awaited Soane in Jezar. There he was challenged by policemen to produce his Turkish issue *tezkere*, or internal visa, and, on doing so, was accused of having stolen it. The passport, besides attesting to British nationality, which contradicted the protestations of Haji Vali, who believed him to be Persian, suggested that Soane was a Protestant. Why, as the policeman asked, did not Soane have a 'Muhammedan' name? Only his wits and the 'feeblest bluff' now saved Soane:

'As to the name,' I said, 'the English law recognizes only surnames; if you are a native of Mosul, are you not called a Mosulli wherever you go? Are you not known among strangers as "the Mosulli"? So I am described as of "Elisun", which is my native place. As to Haji's assertion that I am a Persian, why, that is right enough, are there not thousands of Persians born British subjects? And God knows why the Kafir, the heathen Armenian clerk of the passport department in Constantinople, called me Protestant, except that seeing I was an English subject, imagined that, as the English nation is Protestant, I must be also of that schism.'

Having then submitted his British passport for examination, Soane felt 'doubly triumphant, for I had proved the disguise of languages, manners I had adopted, almost too perfect, and had, at the same time, demonstrated to a crowd of unattached roughs and Turks, that bullying could not extort from me the money which was the sole object of the policeman'. The *kalak*, having crashed heavily and awkwardly in the racing torrent, began to break up, forcing Soane and several others to dive overboard and make for the shore and, with some relief, they realised that at last they were approaching Mosul.

Like Constantinople, Soane found Mosul a 'squalid city on the verge of disintegration', but was struck by its antiquity and racial diversity, and was equally impressed by its exotic odours. It was a rough, dilapidated wilderness place, which Soane was eager to leave for the fabled Zagros Mountains, his temporary idleness rendered acceptable by excellent dates and buffalo cream. Travelling with new companions to Kirkuk via Erbil and Altun Keupri, Soane began to encounter various Kurdish tribes and sects. He was enchanted by the Kurds and by Kurdistan. The country, he claimed, was similar to the medieval Scottish Highlands: inaccessible peaks, dangerous passes and thundering rivers. The people were too often characterised thus: 'little known, feared by his neighbours, a slayer of Christians, merciless in the raid and morose in peace, a creature of lowering brow and dark thoughts, a hater of government and a lover of strife'. Elsewhere, Soane noted, 'In a word, Kurd, moustachios, cloak, and bloodstained dagger complete the costume in which most travellers dress him for popular display.'

Yet, as Soane observed, these were merely stage properties. Their language was especially neglected, something that Soane himself later remedied in several books and articles on Kurdish grammar. Although Soane was by no means the first British officer or traveller from any country to visit Kurdistan, he was undoubtedly its keenest student. He was, moreover, quite willing to face danger in his quest: 'the acquisition of Kurdish in Kurdistan is no easy task, and there have been times when it has been uncertain whether the seeker would not be left with his trove to stiffen upon the cold hills of Kurdistan'.

In the colourful city of Kirkuk, among Jews, Arabs, Syrians, Armenians, Chaldeans, Turks, Turkomans and Kurds, Soane found lodgings in a caravanserai, of all things, next to an agent for Singer's Sewing Machines. Again, Soane's identity was questioned, on this occasion by a servant of the Persian Consul. Anticipating such problems, Soane had prepared his Foreign Office passport, accompanied by visas from both the Persian and Turkish Consuls in London. On each of these, Soane had added his alias, Mirza Ghulam Husain, in indelible ink. Satisfying as this ruse and his popularity with his new acquaintances were, Soane found the heat oppressive. Inactivity was deemed wise because Hamavand raiders lurked nearby; and, whilst the folk music and entertainment offered by the city were some compensation, Soane's expression of deep distaste when he witnessed flies swarming in a butcher's shop, were symptomatic of a need for a cooler and clearer air and, most of all, for action.

At last, amid a long, heavily guarded caravan that snaked among vulture-ridden and parched scenery, Soane made for Sulaimania. En route, the party was intercepted by Hamavands and spent an uneasy night under their guard. However, Soane found them brave and honourable and a pleasant contrast to the backwardness of Sulaimania. There, Soane found a people cocooned by esoteric and conservative social customs and laws that strictly regulated dress and behaviour. Soane quickly grasped the need to assimilate and adopted the guise of a merchant, Mirza Ghulam Husain of Shiraz. In this disguise, Soane secured an introduction to Uthman Pasha of Halabja who, with his 'fierce and cruel' expression and his equally savage guards, presented a terrifying spectacle. Though propriety prevented him from any familiarity with this chieftain, Soane had already befriended several fellow travellers and endured, on their part, tearful farewells when their ways had parted. In fact, whatever his detractors thought of him, there was no doubting Soane's ability to provoke strong reactions in people. Those who spent some time with him appeared generally to admire him greatly. One exception, an Army officer in Kurdistan, had dealings both with Soane and with another intelligence officer, Captain Edward Noel, who replaced Soane, and greatly preferred Noel. In his view, Soane never seemed pleased to see him, invariably treated him with contempt, and he therefore disliked being anywhere near him.

Certainly, Soane was a determined man and did not suffer fools. Making for Halabja, he had a further taste of action. A military escort accompanied the large caravan and Soane's patience was evidently wearing thin with Turkish soldiery. He noted that the duty of these escorts 'seemed to . . . begin and end with a practical study of the science of combined annoyance and roguery, theft and violence'. In an encounter just outside Sulaimania, the escort, fearful of a Hamavand attack, fired on some friendly Kurds and was then set upon and soundly beaten for it. Later, the group sighted a party of raiders and, amid 'wind, thunder, rain, scorpions, [and] regiments of fleas', sheltered overnight behind some makeshift barricades.

Rather different conditions awaited Soane in Halabja, the home of Adela Khanum and her sons of the Jaf Kurds. Lady Adela was an 'extraordinary woman', a 'woman unique in Islam in the power she possesses'. As her guest, Soane was treated with great kindness and respect. He, in turn, was immensely impressed by her leadership and by her intoxicating exoticism. Soane certainly had an eye for beauty and his narrative includes several references to 'saucy Kurdish maids' with 'Turbans cocked at a rakish angle' and suchlike. Yet Soane was also impressed by the fact that Kurdish society appeared to provide some measure of equality to women, in contrast to the harsh oppression endured by Turkish women.

Yet Soane's stay in Halabja was not altogether safe. A bitter and jealous retainer of Lady Adela, who, though born in Constantinople, was German by origin, attempted to expose Soane, now for convenience disguised as a doctor. More worrying was the arrival of the Sheikh ul Islam, a priest whom Soane had befriended in Constantinople when in European dress and who might at any time expose him. Soane decided that if the priest did challenge him he would reply that he had adopted European dress for sake of convenience. Such was Soane's fear of exposure that he went to the priest and, having been robbed and stabbed by a brigand in the process, was obliged to admit to the status of a Persian renegade and a liar in order to pacify the priest. Besides this incident, in the 'secluded and peaceful life' of Lady Adela's inner circle, Soane enjoyed a quiet interlude. Now disguised as a trader, he undertook secretarial duties for Lady Adela, and dressed distinctively in an old pair of pyjamas and dressing gown. In fact, the position suited Soane very well as it enabled him to study the Kurdish people, their culture and their language from a position of relative safety and comfort.

Yet danger was never distant. Turkish police again questioned Soane's identity. Summoned to the Commissaire of Police, Soane found a 'fat man with a cunning look in his little blue eyes, and his mouth concealed under a heavy yellow moustache'. Soane stuck to his story but the commissaire was not convinced by the worn and illegible documents that Soane presented to him. Soane, having demanded to see the governor, was marched off, hand in hand with the policeman. The 'Tabur Aghassi' who interviewed Soane, was another 'fat Turk' but, unlike the policeman, was literate. An examination of Soane's British passport, albeit upside-down, and of the impression of various Turkish stamps, convinced him of Soane's bona fides. Soane, having delighted some Kurdish onlookers with a flagrant display of disrespect towards the Turkish regime, left with a final insult to be greeted by his friends 'as one who had escaped from certain disaster by a rare and wonderful luck'. Having survived a further attempt by the Sheikh ul Islam to denounce him, Soane decided to leave for Baghdad. After many painful farewells, Soane, equipped with a cotton quilt, some road bread and some pears, left Sulaimania.

Soane's hot-headedness, usually with Turkish police or soldiers, was startling and it was a trait that he documented on other occasions. Having reached Kirkuk, perilously famished after exhausting marches, Soane had decided to adopt the guise of a Christian, to see how they were treated in the region. Having been befriended by some Christians, he was clearly disgusted by their habitual overindulgence with food and wine and their nightly 'transition from staid merchants to boisterous idiots'. Similarly, having dragged himself, fevered and weak, to a coffee house, Soane argued with the owner, who refused to let Soane drink warm milk without coffee. Soane exploded and hurled the coffee into his face.

Having twice dodged bullets and the loud and unexpected greetings of Muslim acquaintances, Soane boarded a *kalak* at Altun Keupri and, being roasted like a kebab by the intense heat as it revolved slowly towards Baghdad, contemplated his arrival there and his inevitable re-entry into European society. Behind some bales of straw, Soane changed into a suit, covering it with his dressing gown. Having re-emerged into the world of the

Ferangi, Soane found it wanting: the chairs were hard and the food unpalatable:

> I felt stranger and more lonely than I had done ever before. Gone was the coffee-house and the bazaar, of the multitudes of which I was one and equal, with whom I spoke and laughed, and fought and wrangled. They were far away, and I must leave to look upon them as upon strange and inferior beings.

After this unhappy reversion to European mode, in September 1909 Soane reappeared in Mohammerah in southern Persia, his movements anxiously plotted by the British Military Attaché in Tehran. The Foreign Office shared these concerns but was also aware of Soane's special knowledge and qualifications. These were first brought to bear in a semi-official capacity when Soane, under the guidance of Arnold Wilson, then British Consul in Mohammerah, prepared the first of several reports on southern Kurdistan. The report, like its successors, was highly detailed and covered the government, people, language, culture, religion, topography and other natural features of the country. In fact, the level of Soane's expertise demonstrated in these reports, contributed greatly to his rehabilitation in official eyes. They were variously described as 'first class', 'of great interest and value', 'very carefully compiled'; and, in one case, Soane was thanked for his efforts with a 'handsome cabinet of cutlery'. More significantly, perhaps, it also meant that when, several years later, the Turco-Persian Boundary Commission was undertaking investigations, Soane was asked to accompany them and guide their deliberations on a section of their route.

During this period of writing, Soane's life had taken another twist. As he settled to write his report, Soane was offered employment with Messrs Strick, Scott & Co., agents of the Anglo-Persian Oil Company (APOC). He was apparently taken under the wing of its managing director, Charles Greenway, although this was seemingly not the case with every new recruit to the company. As Greenway noted in connection with another entrant, he was 'not the stamp we want at all. He has no appearance, and his only experience has been 6/7 years with Goetz & Co. (S. Africa), and 1 year as Secretary to Abid the ex-dancing boy of the Nizam and acrobat who was connected with the Jacob diamond case, and otherwise made himself unpleasantly notorious.'

In the winter of 1910/11, Soane and Greenway journeyed to Chiah Surkh to try to secure company property and oil that had fallen into the hands of an unscrupulous notable, Karim Khan. Life was certainly not easy at Mohammerah either. In August 1910, some Indian labourers seriously assaulted Soane and several colleagues. More danger loomed. Posted to Kasr-i-Shirin by APOC, Soane was required to calm the situation in nearby Chiah Surkh. The company had previously allowed Karim to exploit several wells until the company returned. This was in exchange for Karim guarding the wells and paying taxes. Karim now refused to hand back the wells and equipment and threatened with death any Persians who turned up to work for Soane. This was backed up by cruelty and extortion and Soane was soon effectively surrounded by Karim's horsemen and with no food supplies. Meanwhile, Greenway had been vigorously lobbying the British Embassy in Tehran and the Foreign Office itself to have Soane appointed Vice-Consul at Kasr-i-Shirin. Vested with this authority, and possibly with an escort, Greenway and Soane felt that the company's property and Soane himself would be secure. Otherwise, Greenway noted, Soane was in a 'very jeopardous position'. As the situation worsened, senior figures were drawn into the debate. Barclay, the British Ambassador in Tehran, felt unable to recommend Soane – a view shared by one Foreign Office official concerned by Soane's earlier 'delinquencies'. By 26 May, Soane telegraphed urgently: 'Kerim Khan violently preventing our people from selling produce [of wells]. The Persian Government is openly defied by him therefore I have no support. I am maintaining firm attitude.'

This plea followed a tour in which Soane, delirious with fever, had marched for days and, when unable to continue, had then been carried to a meeting with Daud Khan, chief of the Kalhur tribe, who apparently supported the lawless state created by Karim Khan's revolt. Duad Khan had himself annexed large tracts of land, thereby threatening APOC activities. As Soane also recorded, that success was equally threatened by the 'insouciant extravagance' of his predecessor at Chia Surkh, with his staff of 'petulant spendthrifts'. Not only was Soane faced with physical danger but routinely with extortion. At the Foreign Office, senior officials were beginning to soften to the idea of Soane as a vice-consul. Greenway had reported very favourably on him, noting his 'ability and tact in dealing with Persians', and his standing as a 'learned oriental scholar with an intimate knowledge of Persian'. Sir Louis Mallet of the Foreign Office was impressed with the tale of Soane's journey in disguise, with his reputedly strong character, with his alleged consanguinity with Sir John Soane, the famed architect, and with his alleged straightforwardness in all his dealings. On the other hand, as a senior India Office official commented, Soane, if vested with such gifts, 'ought to have been clever enough to commit adultery with impunity'. At any rate, convinced of the seriousness of the situation and the reformed character of Soane, Mallet and the Foreign Secretary himself, Sir Edward Grey, sanctioned Soane's appointment.

Greenway was thankful for this support, albeit of the moral variety, the British government absolving itself of any responsibility should any harm befall Soane. Very soon after his appointment, Soane was indeed exposed to deadly peril. Nearing the Persian frontier one morning on a frequently used road, unarmed and accompanied only by a servant, Soane was shot at by some Turkish guards. As Soane later recalled:

As the bullet knocked up the dust a little way ahead and no one else was in the vicinity, it was obvious that I was their object. I had therefore turned immediately towards the fort and rode slowly towards it, desiring an explanation. Two horsemen at the same moment left the fort and proceeded to right and left of me, while from the fort, despite the fact that I was obviously unarmed and had no intention of escaping, some thirty shots were fired.

Soane was forced to dismount 'with considerable abuse' and his servant's headgear was stolen. The incident, which was taken up personally by Soane in Baghdad and by his employers with the Foreign Office, was apparently linked to Turkish efforts to restrict British crossings of the frontier and at a local level, to the efforts of the governor of Khanikin to obstruct the activities of APOC. Whilst the Foreign Office decided not to make a formal protest, the incident was of sufficient gravity for the Consul-General at Baghdad to be asked to guarantee Soane's safety in future.

Despite periods of serious illness just prior to the war, Soane's extraordinary talents and knowledge were in demand on the outbreak of hostilities. In mid-December 1914, whilst working for APOC in Baghdad, Soane – with forty others, mainly British residents – was taken prisoner by the Turkish authorities. Over the next two months, the 'Baghdad Caravan Party', funded by the American Consul, was escorted to Mersina on the Mediterranean coast, having meandered via Aleppo, Rejou, Osmania, Adana and Tarsous.

At some point after this highly unusual episode, Soane was recruited into the Indian Political Service and was seconded to the staff of Sir Percy Cox, then Chief Political Officer with the British forces in Mesopotamia. 'Pizcox' as Soane called Cox, was an imposing and revered figure in matters relating to the Persian Gulf. He had also, in a previous and more junior incarnation, tried strenuously to debar Soane's entry into those territories in Persia for which he, Cox, had responsibility. By the summer of 1915, however, Cox had revised his opinion of Soane to the extent of personally selecting him for a mission to counter German intrigues in the Bakhtiari country and Arabistan. As Cox recorded at the time, Britain 'could not meet the Germans with diplomacy alone, but must, with limits, use their own methods and weapons'.

However, whilst offering some scope for action, Soane found the company of Indian Army officers trying. C.J. Edmonds, a colleague from this period, noted that he was a man of 'strong opinions and of violent likes and dislikes. Bakhtyaris, Indians, joyriders from GHQ, other uninvited travellers, poor linguists, *effendis*, all were so many red rags to a bull.' In Bakhtiari country in the summer of 1915, Soane moved from his billets rather than tolerate the 'brainless balls about sisi, chikor, markhor, chuppaties, duffadars, pig and my old pals in the 47th pispotspure Lancers'.

This spell of active service and a 'particularly hairy' secret mission for which Soane had been personally nominated by the Grand Duke Nicholas, was broken by a period of relative calm and security for Soane when he was appointed editor of the *Basra Times*. The paper, or its advertising section, was not highly regarded; one particular advertisement, placed by Gray Mackenzie and Company, had for several months in 1915, the year prior to Soane's appointment, advertised the company as 'Agents for Nestlés' Milk, none in stock, but fresh supplies expected within a fortnight'. Soane's successor described the paper as a 'small and modest newspaper . . . which is fed chiefly on Reuter's telegrams, local notices about lawsuits etc. and advertisements'. Essentially a semi-official organ, Soane did much to develop its Persian and Arabic editions that were particularly useful for propaganda purposes.

By September 1916, as Soane noted, his 'kewrious [*sic*] career' in the Political Department was blossoming, having earlier been appointed Assistant Political Officer and Vice-Consul for Dizful. Further postings in the Political Service followed, firstly to take charge of the Khanikin district and then, early in 1919, the Sulaimani district. In Khanikin, however, Soane contracted tuberculosis and a six-month sojourn in Australia failed to effect a complete cure. By 1921, APOC refused to re-employ Soane, who then returned to England to research and write on Kurdish affairs. Two years later, fighting recurrent TB, and en route to England from Tunisia where he had been holidaying, Soane died on board ship.

Yet the strange tale of Ely Soane was not quite over. Throughout the 1920s debate followed about Soane's estate, the bulk of which he had left to St Dunstan's institute for the blind. In September 1918, six months after obtaining leave on account of his ultimately fatal illness, Soane had remarried. His second wife, Lindfield Soane, who became a writer and explorer in the Middle East, was considerably younger than Ely Soane, and had not been living with him prior to his death. In 1929 the Duke of Atholl who, together with several other distinguished men, intervened on her behalf, claimed that Soane had been 'off his head' at the end. In his view, Soane's widow had no choice but to leave Soane to his own devices. She was a 'very good, straight type of woman', an explorer and writer who had acquired something of her husband's ability to get along with Iraqi people. Soane had left her nothing whatsoever in his will yet, for some reason, she had not contested it at the time. After heated and protracted correspondence between government departments it was finally resolved that, as Soane had contracted tuberculosis before they were married, Lindfield Soane was to be denied a pension of any kind.

How spies disguise themselves (disguise at a railway station)

3

Travels in the 'Dark Places of the Earth'

OMINOUS RUMBLINGS IN OUR AFRICAN POSSESSIONS

On the morning of 7 November 1924, a group of senior British officials met in secret session at the India Office. Among them was Sir Vernon Kell, head of the British Security Service, MI5; representatives from the Secret Intelligence Service, MI6; the Indian Intelligence Service, IPI; and others from the Colonial, India, War and Foreign Offices. The meeting – of the Interdepartmental Committee on Eastern Unrest – focused chiefly on the spread of extreme Islamic sympathies from Arabia and the Anglo-Egyptian Sudan to the northern provinces of Nigeria. The urgency of the matter was reflected in the presence at the meeting of Herbert Palmer, a senior official of the Nigeria Service and an expert on Islam in that country.

As the committee listened with rapt attention, Palmer outlined the nature of the problem. Investigations conducted in Nigeria and the Sudan suggested that Nigerian Muslims were particularly susceptible to the extremist Wahabite Muslim doctrine to which they were increasingly exposed on frequent pilgrimages to Mecca in the Hejaz. The centre of this and other extreme movements was held to be the Al Azhar University in Cairo, where some Nigerian students obtained instruction, principally in Theology. The university had been under scrutiny by British officials for some time and Cairo was seen as containing 'hot-beds of intrigue and international espionage'. In order to prevent the subversion of the Nigerian students, and as a means of obtaining further information on broader extremist Islamic currents, the committee resolved to appoint an officer, well acquainted with Nigerian languages and politics – and who might therefore get close to Nigerians – to spend several months in Egypt and the Sudan. G.J. Lethem of the Nigeria Service, who was about to proceed on leave via Darfur and the Anglo-Egyptian Sudan, was duly selected for this highly secret mission. Lethem, an officer of 'marked ability', with a considerable knowledge of Arabic, was to avoid all official contacts but would have special access to the diplomatic bag at Cairo for the transmission of urgent information to Whitehall. Lethem was to conduct himself with discretion and to adopt the mien of a colonial official on vacation. In short, the committee hoped that Lethem would gather much valuable information on anti-British movements which would be useful to both the Nigerian and Sudan governments.

Gordon Lethem was not the first British official to undertake such investigations. Nor was it the first occasion on which a Mahdist uprising had attracted the attention of the Nigerian Service. In order to understand the concerns of the Committee on Eastern Unrest, it is necessary to go back to the first months of 1919. Then, amid similar fears about Mahdism, and on the pretext of establishing a route for two Muslim schoolmasters to travel from Khartoum to Nigeria, H.R. Palmer had himself travelled from Maidugari in northern Nigeria to Jeddah in the Arabian Peninsula, spending five weeks' leave in Egypt en route. Prior to this, another officer of the Nigerian Service, Hans Vischer, had walked from the Mediterranean coast to Bornu, thereafter taking up intelligence duties with MI5 for the remainder of the First World War. In 1919, Palmer had hoped to gather intelligence on an extremely broad range of matters, among them communications, trade, and tribal configurations in the large triangle of territory between northern Nigeria, Khartoum and Cairo. On the latter issue, in his report Palmer had emphasised that the population in large parts of Chad had long-standing connections with the Shehus of Bornu and that they regarded tribal leaders in Bornu as the 'real heads of their units'. The lack of commercial development by France, the colonial power in Chad, meant that it was, in Palmer's view, little more than an appendage of neighbouring British possessions. Moreover, the laissez-faire attitude of the Anglo-Egyptian authorities towards unorthodox spiritual forces led Palmer to believe that significant numbers in Chad, but also in parts of northern Nigeria, might be drawn to the Sudan. According to Palmer, the adoption of tolerant policies among Muslim communities in Nigeria, and the institution of economic improvements in the Bornu Province and in parts of Chad would alone check this trend.

Further east, in the Wadai region, Palmer encountered tribes, 'half Negro and half Arab in origin', who, fortified by strong drink, harboured a 'fanatical hatred of the European' unsurpassed elsewhere in the Sudan belt. These sentiments were, in Palmer's view and that of native opinion, largely due to the 'bureaucratic, inquisitorial, and highly centralised' French administration. As Palmer continued, native preachers or *mallams* actively taught that the murder of a European assured salvation:

> Though the most elaborate precautions are taken for the safety of Europeans – in Abeshe itself no European moves out of his house without an armed guard – there are found natives who are ready to face certain death if they can make quite sure of gaining immortal reward by a successful assassination. It is at the present moment a measure of prudence on the part of any European not to allow a Wadai to come near him unless he is quite sure that he has not a knife about his person. Feigning sick, a bogus complaint, or a mere profession of a desire to salute, are the methods adopted to get within striking distance of a European, and it is quite common along the road to catch muttered or open expressions such as 'Uktul al abiadth' – 'Kill the white!'

In the Kordofan region, Palmer's investigations revealed striking similarities between the Arab peoples and vegetation and those of

Bornu; although, apparently, little evidence of communications between those peoples. However, communication clearly was taking place between groups of the Takarir (émigré West Africans) elsewhere in the Sudan and their brethren in Nigeria. Having traversed the Sudan and reached Jeddah, Palmer found the Takarir exposed to degrading conditions and to the scorn and contempt of the Hejaz Arabs, and torn between their religious devotion on the one hand and hatred of the Arab and the privations of Arabia on the other.

*   *   *

In submitting his report, Palmer emphasised that his findings had to be seen in the context of the effect of the First World War upon the territories that he had traversed. War had exposed many communities to European lifestyles and ideas and in Palmer's view there was a risk of Black African aspirations developing into a broad-based anti-Europeanism. A key antidote to this, and to the emergence of extremist Mahdist 'incendiary preachers', was the maintenance of settled native hierarchies and respect on the part of the British administration towards native *ulemas* and religious practices.

Palmer's journey had taken him across some of the least-known territory in northern Africa and had involved considerable risk. Among other things, he had to cross a particularly dangerous river by means of a ferry. As it proceeded, a man played a flute in order to charm the *jinn* or, as Palmer correctly detected, a strong undertow. He ventured through villages where the entire population was incapably drunk and into the Wadai region, where there had in recent years been repeated assassinations of French officers. Exactly what he would find or what dangers he might encounter were unknown. Intercepted correspondence between Egyptians, Sudanese and Nigerians seemed to suggest that, since the end of the war, propaganda hostile to Britain was being disseminated in a more systematic way. Several groups had emerged, including the committees of the 'White Hand and Black Hand', and the 'Committee of Urgent Affairs'. There were signs of interest in the nature and strength of British control in Nigeria and signs also of other potentially hostile groups in North Africa being drawn into these discussions. It was not without reason that one official remarked that, but for Palmer's efforts at intelligence gathering in 1919 and over the next few years, a Mahdist rising might have 'flashed right across Central Africa'.

However, Palmer's enthusiasm for a vigilant approach towards signs of unrest was not uniformly popular with colleagues in the Nigeria Service. One superior at the Colonial Office, G.L.M. Clauson, who routinely attended meetings of the Committee on Eastern Unrest, at least regarded Palmer as more convincing than did those who had not personally travelled in and experienced the cruelties of the 'dark places of the earth'. Whatever the reality of the threat to Nigeria, Palmer's journey had come about because of signs that the settled conditions necessary to withstand unrest were in jeopardy. On the outbreak of war with Turkey in the autumn of 1914 and for several months afterwards, indications were almost uniformly to the effect that Britain had no reason to fear for the loyalties of her most important Nigerian Muslim subjects. Quite simply they did not identify with the distant caliph in Constantinople. However, other developments were afoot that were to alarm the British authorities.

* * *

From 1900 the Nigerian colonial authorities had been broadly supportive of Christian missionary activity among independent pagan communities, even where those communities included small settlements of Muslims. Nor did the British authorities prohibit missionary efforts in communities ruled by Muslim emirs provided that those communities were large and homogenous. Their serious objection was to unbridled evangelising among small numbers of pagans scattered among significant Muslim communities. In short, it was felt that such activities, if identified with the British administration, would contravene repeated assurances given to emirs of a 'hands-off' policy with regard to religious matters. Apart from anything else, it was deemed likely to interfere with the introduction of government-sponsored schooling.

Well before the outbreak of war in 1914, intelligence revealed that missionaries were targeting Muslims and that this was leading to disturbances. There was also evidence of individual missionaries attempting to subvert pro-British sentiments in parts of Nigeria. In 1913, the governor of Nigeria, Sir Henry Lugard, had agreed to cooperate in a survey of the spread of Islam in Nigeria conducted by the Committee of the World Missionary Conference. Whilst the Colonial Office feared a 'campaign against Islam', the missionary societies suspected the British authorities of encouraging and subsidising the instruction of Muslims in the Koran, and of imposing unfair restrictions upon their proselytising activities. The Colonial Office was determined to channel missionary endeavours in appropriate directions. In January 1917, Charles Strachey of the Colonial Office informed the Church Missionary Society that he had evidence of the 'highly injudicious' behaviour of members of the society in northern Nigeria. As Strachey pointed out, if this behaviour led to injury or death, the British government would be duty-bound to avenge it, and this in turn would provoke native opposition and unrest. The society and its members should remember, Strachey intoned, that the Muslim world was deeply involved in, and deeply divided by, the war, and Britain's enemies were actively promoting a holy war. Most of Britain's Nigerian troops were Muslim and the relatively low number of British troops in Nigeria itself were Muslim.

Palmer, writing shortly after this interview, detected other disturbing currents at work. Previously, Nigerian Muslims had been largely unaffected by the propagandising efforts of Germans, Turks and followers of the Senussi. By 1917, the proximity of Nigeria to groups of devout Muslims in adjoining areas of the Sahara, in Chad and in the Sudan, threatened to counteract this isolation. Ruthless French suppression of outbreaks in the Sahara and their conscription of Sudanese to fight in France, led Palmer to fear a ripple effect undermining British relations with her Muslim Nigerian subjects. As an antidote, especially in the fanatical areas of French Chad and in parts of the Sudan, Palmer felt that the authorities must encourage stable tribal life under reliable emirs and chiefs.

Those who questioned Palmer's call for vigilance were jolted into reality by events in Nyasa in the Sudan in September 1921. According to the monthly Sudan intelligence report,

> At about 8:30am on 26 September, insurgents, whose numbers were estimated at 5,000, with nine flags, advanced in a solid phalanx from the south. . . . By sheer force of numbers, and in spite of heavy casualties from rifle fire, the attack succeeded in penetrating the defences. Captain Chown emptied his revolver and then seized a rifle, which jammed. He was then surrounded and died fighting gallantly inside the square. Mr McNeill, the inspector, rallied the retreating troops and police and made a gallant stand, but he and they were forced slowly backwards through the fortified area, and he died 150 yards to the north of it pierced by four spears.

The rising came as a shocking reminder of General Gordon's fate in 1885. Besides European casualties, several Sudanese government officials and troops from the Western Arab Corps had perished. The rising had been sudden and came with little warning. On investigation, it was clear that the administration had for long been regarded as too invasive and there was evidence of the circulation in the Sudan of hostile propaganda. The propaganda itself revealed close links with malcontents in Egypt. Chiefly it focused on the accusation that Christian countries had conspired during the war to crush Islam. Egyptian nationalists had also made contact with Sudanese Muslims and, in return for their support, had offered them an independent Sudan. Intelligence collected by the Sudan authorities indicated that this propaganda was also affecting West African settlements in the Sudan itself. This was particularly alarming because many of these groups were followers of the Mahdi and it was above all to a resurgence of the Mahdist movement and propaganda that the Sudan government attributed the Nyasa rising and broader currents of unrest.

Essentially, Mahdism was a belief among orthodox Sunni Muslims that, as the precursor of the second coming of Christ and of the millennium, God would send the Rightly Guided One (*el Mahdi*). His emergence would herald the deliverance of the world from evil and a reign of perfect justice. By the outbreak of war in 1914, Abdel Rahman-el-Mahdi, son of Mohammed Ahmad, the Mahdist leader whose revolt in the 1880s had overthrown British rule in the Sudan, was generally recognised as leader by followers of the Mahdi. During the first years of the war, Rahman cooperated with the British authorities in spreading anti-Turkish propaganda and he was able to consolidate his position both in financial terms and as heir to the Mahdist tradition. By 1921–2, information suggested that Mahdist propaganda was widespread throughout Kordofan and Darfur in the Sudan. Efforts from December 1921 to restrict Rahman's agents failed to curb their disruptive effects on stable tribal discipline.

Some Mahdist propaganda taught that Rahman would shortly reveal himself as the Prophet Jesus and that he would overthrow the government. Worse still, in line with the belief that the second coming of Christ would be preceded by the appearance of the anti-Christ, some propagandist tracts identified this figure with the British official. In May 1923, a pilgrimage estimated at between 5,000 and 15,000 gathered on Abu Island, sacred because of its associations with Mohammed Ahmad. The government responded by summoning Rahman to Khartoum, where he was instructed to disperse the pilgrims, and by asking governors throughout the country to discourage further pilgrimages. Sir John Maffey reinforced these measures in 1926 when he became Governor-General of the Sudan.

These developments in the Sudan would not have been of particular significance for the Nigerian authorities had it not been for further investigations undertaken in the spring of 1923 by H.R. Palmer. Returning from leave late in 1922, Palmer was directed urgently to investigate religious propaganda in parts of northern Nigeria. On arrival in Maidugari, Palmer learned of the existence there of a manuscript believed to be of great importance, which inhabitants were paying to see. Hastening to view it, Palmer discovered that it was a Mahdist tract, urging the faithful to prosecute a holy war against Europeans. More worrying still, when Palmer interviewed and subsequently imprisoned the instigator of this propaganda, one Mallam Sa'id, it emerged that he was in direct correspondence with Abdel Rahman. Early communications between Sa'id and Rahman suggested that the former, whose father Rahman had appointed Sultan of Sokoto, wished to be confirmed in that position, to renew his pledges of support and loyalty, and to continue his Mahdist propaganda activities. Further investigations revealed that this correspondence had persisted since 1919 and that it was 'highly seditious and violently anti-Christian'. Reports of unusual Mahdist practices reached Palmer, such as worshippers praying for five days in a week, hands resting on the chest or behind the back when in prayer, and the wearing of colourful dresses by prominent worshippers, Mallam Sa'id among them. Further intercepted correspondence also indicated support for Mallam among influential Fulani emirs and others in many areas of Nigeria. There were rumours of Mahdist activities in neighbouring French territories and troops left for Maidugari after Mahdist missionaries had interfered with Mallam's arrest. It was at this critical moment that the whole issue was referred back to London and to the Interdepartmental Committee on Eastern Unrest.

By the end of 1924, the nature of Lethem's mission had crystallised. In his highly secret instructions, he was asked to compile an extremely broad report, which 'could hardly . . . be too detailed', based upon a diary kept on the road. The report would encompass not only the physical character of the territory being traversed but also the anthropological and ethnographical features of its indigenous populations. In addition to analysing the relative merits of the various routes from Nigeria to the Sudan, Lethem was to study the racial affinities, customs, trade, languages, and political and social outlook of tribes encountered. In particular, he was to be watchful when among Muslim communities, especially with regard to religious practices and beliefs, the survival or otherwise of indigenous forms of government, and attitudes towards other Muslim and African communities. Specifically, Lethem was to 'pay very special attention to any communities or individuals of Nigerian origin or descent' and to their 'social, economic and political conditions'. Information about the pilgrim traffic was specially prized and Lethem was also required to observe the dynamics of nomadic groups encountered on the way.

As a relative novice in intelligence gathering, Lethem's instructions emphasised that, if he should form definite opinions on particular matters, he must provide evidence for these judgements. However, as a mark of the importance of the mission, Lethem was permitted to communicate direct with the Sudanese authorities and, by means of the diplomatic bag in Khartoum, with the British Foreign Office, and he was to request the assistance of the French authorities at Fort Lamy in communications between the Sudan and Nigeria. The degree of importance attached to Lethem's mission was also underlined in further highly confidential instructions which were conveyed to him on the same day. The main object of his mission was to assess the extent, nature, origin, and effect of religious or political propaganda in the countries to be traversed. Lethem was to prolong his stay at any time should this yield further intelligence and, as his instructions continued, 'you should divest yourself . . . of your official character, and should assume as far as may be feasible the rôle of an officer on leave who has a taste for wandering, and who is interested in anthropological studies and especially in all matters relating to Muhammadans and to the Muhammadan religion'. Lethem was permitted a small retinue of native followers and was to be rigorous in his analysis of influences among Nigerian travellers in the east, but also in checking and cross-checking information supplied to him.

The Mallam Sa'id episode revealed serious concerns about Britain's lack of understanding of and response to subversive movements throughout North and West Africa. It was also felt that more could be done to improve cooperation with the French colonial authorities. As the extent of east–west subversive connections emerged with Palmer's investigations in 1923, the Foreign Office insisted that Sudanese intelligence summaries should be sent to the Nigerian authorities. An analysis of these and other documents by the Nigerian authorities convinced them that their counterparts in the Sudan – and in particular the head of intelligence, C.A. Willis – had not attached due importance to the Mahdist outbreaks in Nigeria. Willis's argument that much of the trouble stemmed from the return of the Takarir to Nigeria after the *Haj* with tales of the imminent collapse of western civilisation was not seen as convincing by the Nigerian authorities. Willis believed that Abdel Rahman was not deeply involved in the spread of Mahdist tenets but that this was chiefly the work of *fiki*, or priests, whom he was unable effectively to control. Willis and his superiors also ascribed some of the unrest to activities of Mahdist supporters at the Al Azhar University in Cairo.

The Sudanese and Nigerian authorities agreed that the absence of outward signs of unrest did not mean that it did not exist on a subterranean level, and it was this assumption, coupled with anxieties about the true extent of the unrest, that led to the referral of the matter to the Eastern Unrest Committee late in

1924. To W.J. Gowers, Lieutenant-Governor of northern Nigeria, it was a 'smouldering fire, never totally extinguished, which may at any time, set ablaze the mass of inflammable Moslem sentiment'. However, besides concerns about the response of the Sudanese authorities to the problem, the Nigerian authorities and some Foreign Office officials in London were less inclined than Willis to regard the Nigerian and Sudanese Mahdist outbreaks as localised affairs. If anything, their investigations pointed to the existence of broader conspiracies. As an example of this, investigations by SIS into the source of the paper on which the Mahdist propaganda in Nigeria was written led to the Cordenone Mill in Italy, which exported significant quantities to the Sudan. The same mill also appeared to be supplying the paper for propaganda emanating from Egypt and Beirut.

A key figure in attempting to place the Nigerian and Sudanese outbreaks in a broader context was Francis Rodd of the Foreign Office, who had previously been employed on military intelligence duties in the Middle East. Writing in June 1924, Rodd, who had himself explored the region, had emphasised the need to establish effective reporting mechanisms for British Consuls throughout North Africa. Although he did not fear an imminent pan-Islamic explosion, he detected a very broad upsurge of nationalism from French West Africa through Morocco, Algeria, Tunisia and encompassing the entire Nigerian–Sudanese belt. This nationalism frequently took the guise of religious movements and, whilst there were real stumbling blocks to anything resembling widespread and co-ordinated unrest, many if not most of these groups of malcontents had connections with each other. Besides the Sudan, Rodd detected two other centres of trouble, namely the Fezzan and Morocco. In addition, whatever religious or ethnographical impediments might exist to a wider upheaval, Rodd considered the east–west Mahdist or anti-European movement to be of the 'gravest importance'. In particular, he felt that the French in North Africa were 'sitting on a very live volcano'. More broadly,

Rodd anticipated that the influence of the Mahdist and Senussi movements would increase. Whilst cooperation between those movements was unlikely, Rodd feared – and with good reason – that, in the event of Mahdist unrest in northern Nigeria, the Senussi would provoke unrest among the nomadic and anti-French Tuareg, who would then act as conduits for unrest further to the north.

Lethem's investigations in the Sudan, Egypt and the Hejaz confirmed fears that Willis and his intelligence department in Khartoum had underestimated the involvement of Abdel Rahman and that, in general, they had failed to counter Mahdist intrigues. Having run to earth the 'one-eyed Shuaibu' and extracted a confession that he had acted as go-between in the Mallam Sa'id–Abdel Rahman correspondence, Lethem had also gathered detailed information about the nature of Mahdist settlements on the Blue Nile.

According to Lethem's intelligence gathering, the existence of these settlements owed much to migration from Nigeria in the aftermath of unrest there in 1902–3 and very little to commercial inducements or to more recent religious propaganda or unrest. Owing to the scarcity of the indigenous Sudanese population, these settlements of Nigerians or West Africans were correspondingly noticeable and were also notable, in contrast to the Sudanese, for their desire to complete the *Haj*, or pilgrimage to Mecca, which lies in modern Saudi Arabia. This had produced a substantial population that was neither strictly settled nor transitory and, because of economic and social factors, tended to remain in this state of limbo for many years. Many would-be pilgrims on reaching the Sudan had to find work in order to afford the payment of passage through the country, then to Jeddah by boat, and through the Hejaz quarantine.

With great skill and presence of mind, Lethem managed to infiltrate the Mahdist communities of the Blue Nile. On one occasion at least, he was certainly helped by the attendance of his wife, who reported enthusiastically on a tea party given for her husband by Mai Wurno, fifth son of At Tahiru, the supposed martyr of the unrest in 1903. On that occasion, Lethem and his wife were treated to ginger beer and biscuits. Lethem found these Blue Nile Mahdists to be more forthcoming than their counterparts on the White Nile. As he reported later, he had little doubt that this was the focus of Mahdism and that the communities had gathered there around Mai Wurno and at the instigation of Mahdist agents. Lethem found Mai Wurno physically unprepossessing but intelligent, scheming, and prepared to abuse his authority. According to Lethem, the activities of the Blue Nile communities acted as a 'leaven which has kept alive a spirit of religious fanaticism and of unrest among the whole Takarir community in the Sudan'. All of the key Mahdist agitators in the Sudan – Faki Abakr, Ahmadu Dumba, Mohammad Nur Isa and 'Sambo Sambo' – had had links with the Blue Nile communities. Besides Mai Wurno, Lethem also met Ahmadu of Messau, another leading figure among the Takarir. He judged him to be 'lacking in the restraint and dignity which characterises a Nigerian Emir of his standing . . . and probably deficient in the ability to foresee and consider'.

Lethem's investigations convinced him that the problem was one of movement – or, rather, a lack of it among would-be pilgrims. Of the 56,000 West African migrants he estimated to be on the move between Chad and Mecca, roughly 21,000 might be expected to settle permanently in the east. Of an estimated 80,000 West African migrants in the Sudan, Lethem put at 55,000 the number permanently settled there, with an additional floating population of approximately 25,000. Of those 80,000, roughly three-quarters were of Nigerian origin and, in Lethem's estimate, about half of those had left Nigeria prior to 1912. The remaining West African migrants were located in Eritrea and Abyssinia but also in settlements in Jeddah, Medina and Mecca, with Medina providing the best living conditions. Those in Jeddah, whose migratory population tended to remain longer than those elsewhere, either because of crime or impoverishment, were the worst. Having visited one settlement there, Lethem encountered a Nigerian, whom he had previously known as a wealthy Bornu merchant, and who invited him to his quarters. According to Lethem, 'it was a crazy shelter of old grass, patched on one side with an old pair of trousers and on the other side with pieces of rusty kerosene cans and in which one adult might just huddle himself up'.

Lethem was a lawyer by training and he was a stickler for detail and for facts. He freely admitted that he found it extremely difficult to assess the reliability of the intelligence that he gathered. His findings, as he later noted, were based not upon absolute proof but were rather the result of 'general impression and cumulative conviction'. He had heard much 'fantastic and credulous nonsense' and many rabidly anti-western sentiments, but he was emphatic that, in a country such as Nigeria, the rumours could easily and very rapidly become the basis of political movements. In his view and that of Palmer, Britain must not be complacent. It was inevitable that political movements in northern Africa would affect Nigeria. At least some of the hostile propaganda in Nigeria did not emanate from the Sudan but was being spread by Egyptian, Bolshevik, German and Turkish agents. Britain had failed to develop in northern Nigeria a political administration that might withstand these elements and it was partly for this reason that he now faced the singularly dangerous task of entering the Al Azhar mosque itself. If he were to locate the powerhouse of eastern unrest then surely it would be there?

Lethem was well aware of the importance of his mission and the need to turn every stone in order to find the true source of the problem. Consequently, having detected a lull in the more blatantly hostile anti-British propaganda, in the guise of an 'interested tourist', he entered the mosque. As he recalled, a young Berbine student showed him around the premises:

I was most courteously received, and penetrated, as far as I could see, into every corner of the mosque, and into the living and

101

studying rooms of every *ruwak* [nation or section in Al Azhar]. I was shown the manuscripts in the library by the Sheikh in charge, and was entertained to coffee and cigarettes by the registrars, who showed and explained to me the registers and the various certificates issued, and gave me a form showing the divisions into *ruwaks*, and filling in for me the numbers in each.

Lethem was fascinated by the large Turkish, Syrian, Mugharba, and Javan *ruwaks*, and the relatively small size and moribund nature respectively, of the Sudanese and Darfur *ruwaks*. He noted that the Wadai *ruwak*, though composed of only five students, was headed by a sheikh of vehemently anti-European views, and, in some moments of breathless suspense, Lethem even managed to inspect the quarters of the Bornu *ruwak*, rummaging among the assorted boxes and books for signs of propaganda.

In a nine-day visit to Cairo, Lethem discovered that there was a small group ready to act as conduits for the unrest that afflicted the Sudan and Nigeria. He reported that of the 120 or so Nigerians in Cairo, 17 of them studied at Al Azhar, others finding a living as '*bori* dancers, sorcerers, women's doctors, [and] retailers of aphrodisiacs', among other things. Though he actively pursued his enquiries, taking coffee with Nigerian worshippers and discreetly interviewing Nigerians with a reputation for troublemaking, Lethem did not find any main source of propaganda. Some Sudan officials also sensed that Cairo was the centre of the web of intrigue, and that the villain of the piece, the 'organising power' behind the unrest, could only have been one man: Prince Omar Toussoun. According to one official, he was a 'sphinx'. His ambitions were unknown but he was immensely rich, and he was very popular in Egypt. Yet, though he did not unmask Toussoun or indeed any single malevolent influence, Lethem's risk-taking was not entirely fruitless. The head of the Bornu *ruwak*, Sheikh Mohamman Ali ibn Mongali, a British subject and son of an emir deposed by the Nigerian authorities in 1902–3, had previously supplied the Sudan Agency with intelligence, and Lethem took steps to retain his services and to reward him for this information. Lethem also made contact with several Nigerians in Cairo who had a reputation for troublemaking and ensured that those who spoke of returning to Nigeria were closely watched.

Lethem's mission, though inconclusive, was important in several respects. Firstly, he obtained a clearer impression of the nature of the Mahdist threat to Nigeria and the channels through which it worked. Secondly, after discussion among the relevant authorities, some of Lethem's proposed countermeasures were adopted. In order to address the lack of reliable intelligence about the activities of Nigerians in the Hejaz, the British Agent at Jeddah was provided with a small fund by the Nigerian authorities to disburse among his sources of intelligence on this subject. Lethem also proposed measures – eventually sanctioned in 1928 – for the regulation and speeding up of the Nigerian pilgrim traffic by a system of advance payment, the issuing of passports, and the direction of pilgrims along certain routes. Both of these aims were to be facilitated by periodic visits by an officer of the Nigerian Service to the Sudan, Cairo and the Red Sea. Further intelligence was to be obtained from the Sudan Agent in Cairo and the restructured Sudan Intelligence Agency. Although Lethem had found no damning evidence at Al Azhar, it was now clear that British officials throughout Asia had entertained similar suspicions about its unsettling effects on students attending from the countries to which they were posted.

Whatever was expected of Lethem's fact-finding mission, on its completion the broader picture of unrest across North Africa remained unsatisfactory. Reports from Morocco, Algeria and Tunisia generally indicated little evidence in those countries of Mahdist tendencies, and that where unrest existed it was chiefly nationalist and political rather than religious in origin. At the Foreign Office, however, fears persisted of Nigerian Mahdism. Some British Consuls in North Africa perceived this emerging unrest as part of a broader phenomenon sweeping through the east and challenging the old order. Early in 1927, an official at the Foreign Office warned that a resurgence of Mahdism might well originate in Nigeria or in the French Sudan and reach the Anglo-Egyptian Sudan as a 'going concern'. This fear stemmed partly from the recommendations of a subcommittee of the British Committee of Imperial Defence (CID), which had considered the Mahdist threat in the Sudan. The meetings of that body reinforced earlier concerns that the Sudan authorities underestimated the danger posed by Mahdist unrest. In its first report, the committee addressed the issue of possible Mahdist unrest in the broader context of the defence requirements of Sudan. Having consulted widely among intelligence and military sources, the committee concluded that other than sporadic outbreaks, there was little chance of a widespread Mahdist rising in the Sudan itself.

When the committee reported for a second time, late in June 1927, the debate had broadened to encompass the Mahdist threat in Nigeria and the committee decided that it was no longer a 'real danger'. Paradoxically, as the subcommittee of the CID had prepared to meet, Lord Crewe, Britain's Ambassador in Paris, had been instructed to request greater exchange of information and coordinated action with French authorities on the borders of Nigeria. The request came amid evidence that Abdel Rahman's activities were, 'developing in an increasing degree a measure of organisation and coherence'.

These concerns were borne out by an attack conducted from within Nigeria across the border on Tassawa in French territory early in June 1927, in which a Frenchman and two native policemen were killed. The attack, led by a religious recluse who claimed to be Jesus resurrected was, in Lethem's view, linked to a broader recurrence of Mahdist and religious unrest. Added to this was the murder by a religious fanatic – recently returned from the *Haj* – of Assistant District Officer P.W.D. Thurley. Added to these developments, in Zaria and Kano in northern Nigeria, missionary activities had led to complaints and prolonged debates about the proper activities of missionary bodies. Both places had previously been the focus of unrest and, soon after these incidents, Palmer reported a recurrence of this unrest. More broadly, the British High Commission in Cairo had further evidence of links between Bolsheviks and the extreme Egyptian nationalists and evidence that this coalition was meddling in the Hejaz and the Sudan, where it aimed to provoke agitation and unrest. The key perpetrator was said to be Abdel Rahman. This information tied in with evidence of renewed attempts to spread Mahdist propaganda in Nigeria, much of it closely resembling the material previously intercepted by Palmer and Lethem. To Lethem this seemed to bear out his fear that even the most secluded areas of Muslim Africa were no longer immune from the organised forces seeking to spread worldwide revolution. By 1928, the Nigerian authorities were in little doubt that this trend required investigation and to this end, and with the backing of the Colonial Office, they had taken a keen interest in several journeys undertaken by British subjects through West and North Africa. At the Colonial Office, besides a passing sarcasm that Lethem and Palmer were at times inclined to see a Mahdi behind every bush, there was general support for Clauson's belief that the nature of the 'various undercurrents', religious or political, required investigation. It was possible that Nigerian students at Al Azhar might be suborned to the Mahdist cause and, as Clauson noted, Lethem or a colleague might usefully be 'launched on another Trans-African "Cook's Tour"'.

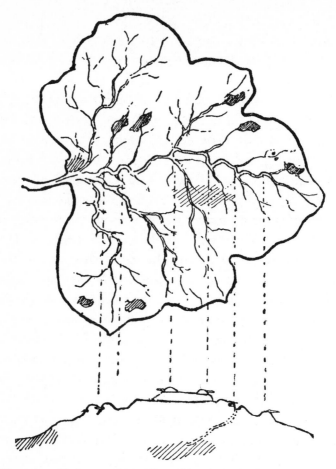

The value of being stupid (outline of fort in ivy leaf)

4

Between the Soviets and the Germans

Towards the end of June 1921, Edwin Montagu, the volatile but brilliant Secretary of State for India, sent an urgent note to the War Office. In a tone bordering on panic, Montagu demanded the attention of his colleagues to the imminent threat from the Russian Bolshevik regime. Their purpose, he continued, was 'to destroy the prestige of the British Empire . . . and to assail our territories in the East'. With the note were two highly secret memoranda which examined the widespread unrest. Their author was N.N.E. Bray (1885–1962). Bray – Indian Army officer, special intelligence operative, SIS man, polyglot, critic of T.E. Lawrence, author of biographical and historical works, later an RAF officer, suspected fascist and gun-runner – is an intriguing figure whose importance in the investigation and analysis of anti-British movements has until recently been overlooked.

After the First World War, as well as having troubles on the domestic labour front, Britain faced nationalist outbreaks in Ireland, Egypt, India and Burma, unrest in Afghanistan, and was hearing the rumblings of Islamic unrest across North Africa. The unrest in Mesopotamia, the mainspring of British strategic and economic interests in the Middle East, was especially disturbing to policy makers. Just when it seemed vital to limit British military commitments there, serious nationalist and tribal unrest erupted among sections of its Arab and Kurdish population. By October 1920 about 60 British Army or Indian Army officers and over 800 other ranks had been killed in this unrest.

Norman Napier Evelyn Bray, like many British officers of his generation, exhibited several characteristics that contributed equally to his success and to his undoing. These were an early contact with India (and connected with it, a solitary schooling in England), a deep Christian belief, a passionate imperialism, a lonely megalomania, and a belief that he had been singled out by Providence for special service in the empire. In Bray's case the factors were sharpened by a measure of real or perceived personal misfortune, social hardship, and emotional neglect in his formative years. For by the time that Bray became an officer cadet, his father had died of disease on active service, his mother had emigrated to Australia and Bray had been left in the care of an Anglican cleric. As he recalled in later life, 'The yearnings I experienced in my lonely watches in India, and my solitary wanderings in Norfolk, were translated into a knowledge and belief and trust in a merciful God.'

Bray first came to the attention of the Foreign Office in the spring of 1913 as a would-be traveller and Arabic scholar in Syria and the Lebanon. He was inspired to undertake the trip by fears of subversion expressed in 1911 by Sir Charles Cleveland, Director of Criminal Intelligence in India. Under the impression that these conspiracies were being hatched and directed from outside India, and that the threat was 'real and deadly', Bray spent almost a year in the Middle East studying the military and political position. There, as an officer of the 18th Lancers, he had contact, either direct or by means of agents, with 'men of influence and standing'. Although he was not formally commissioned to investigate the situation there, Bray chose to develop his knowledge of the pan-Islamic movement and, possibly for this reason, he commenced his journey in Switzerland, the centre of many cabals then as now.

Bray's Syrian adventure was a colourful episode and quite justified the fears at the Foreign Office that his journey was unwise. As Bray later recorded, he was 'dogged by [Turkish] secret service agents; shot at from an ambush . . . and, finally, poisoned with arsenic', only being saved by the attentions of a Polish lady doctor. One evening in June 1914, as he gathered information in Damascus, a German officer – a Major von Hochwaechter – a friend of the Kaiser, had approached Bray. Finding that Bray was headed for India, the Major became 'suspiciously friendly'. Pretending to reciprocate this, Bray drank champagne with him but the Major, who had hoped to get Bray drunk and thereby obtain military secrets, himself succumbed to the alcohol. Bray, anxious to glean any intelligence he could, relieved the Major of a telegram. When he read its contents, he left immediately for England. According to Bray, the telegram had revealed that Germany planned to make war in August 1914. Denied an audience with Sir Edward Grey, and without further leave at his disposal, Bray returned to India. There, more disappointments awaited him. For, on the outbreak of war, his superiors were unwilling to accept his advice that Britain should arm and support Ibn Saud, who later founded the Saudi dynasty, and that he, Bray, who 'knew the whole country and the people', should lead this Arab army and take Damascus. Bray had indeed suggested such a scheme in June 1915, if not earlier, and his thinking at this time was closely aligned with the emerging support, under the auspices of Lord Kitchener, Secretary for War, and Ronald Storrs, Oriental Secretary at the British Embassy in Cairo, for effective British control over large sections of the Arab Middle East. In Syria, Bray had gained the impression that the Arab population believed Britain was about to 'assist in the realization of a permanent independence'. Instead, amid much bickering between departments, the British government decided to support Sheriff, later King, Hussein of the Hejaz, the main rival of Ibn Saud.

By most standards Bray had a 'good' war. After spells of duty in France, he was assigned to a special mission to Sheriff Hussein. On its successful completion Bray was summoned to an audience with King George V in November 1916. As Bray recalled, 'I felt that all the suffering and dangers I had encountered were an insignificant price to pay for such commendation. I determined to dedicate my whole life to this service and, as God is my witness, I have never faltered.'

Almost in the same breath, Bray recalled his subsequent, ill-fated, attachment to the Sykes-Picot Political Mission. As part of the arrangements for supporting the Arab Revolt, Britain and France had sent officers to the Hejaz to establish acceptable division of responsibilities there. Bray was instructed to organise the Arab Legion, an Anglo-French officered body with Arab soldiery recruited mostly from prisoner of war camps. Bray's involvement with the Mission rapidly acquainted him with the true nature of British policy in the region, namely to create a façade of Arab government underpinned by actual British control. Having himself in 1915 advocated strong British control over 'Arabia', broadly defined, his subsequent resignation from the Mission is puzzling. At any rate, that decision apparently cost him the Distinguished Service Order and Military Cross for which he had been recommended.

Before returning to France, where he fought with distinction (and was, in fact, subsequently awarded the MC), Bray came to the attention of the authorities in several ways. In August 1916, in the notorious 'Silk Letters' conspiracy, the Indian authorities intercepted letters revealing plans for a union of Islamic countries against Britain. This conspiracy, spearheaded by the 'Army of God' or Al Junad Al Rabbania, allegedly included Hussein of Mecca, the Sultan of Turkey, the Amir of Afghanistan and the Shah of Persia. As previously noted, Bray was selected to undertake a secret mission to Sheriff Hussein to persuade him that he was at risk of being undermined in the Muslim world by intrigue. Bray had also suggested the despatch of a deputation of Indian Muslim officers from France to Hussein in order to unite Muslim opinion in India, Persia and Afghanistan under the banner of the Arab Revolt. If Hussein were willing, Bray also suggested that Muslim volunteers might then be transported to Jeddah together with hand-picked men from France 'to give confidence and backbone to the Arab revolt'. An appeal of this kind from Hussein would, according to Bray, 'knock the bottom out of the whole pro-Turk propaganda'. This idea gained the backing of senior figures in Whitehall, and it was ostensibly for this reason that, after an interview with Sir Arthur Hirtzel of the India Office, Bray found himself in Jeddah awaiting the return of the mission.

Bray's thinking was in tune with developments in the Arab Revolt and reflected the efforts of several agencies to understand the nature of subterranean movements from the Sudan throughout the Arab Middle East and in India. The coordinating agency in these efforts from the summer of 1916 was the Arab Bureau in Cairo. It solicited reports from various experts including Valentine Vivian, the future deputy head of the SIS, from officers of the Sudan government and Intelligence Department of the East Africa Force, from Sir Charles Cleveland, and from Lt Col Wilson, British Resident at Jeddah.

By September 1916, British authorities in the Middle East and in London feared for the success of the revolt. Turkish forces were outmanoeuvring Arab forces to make a direct assault on Mecca to coincide with the annual pilgrimage. However, Hussein was emphatic that no Christian troops should be landed on the sacred soil of the Hejaz. Various solutions were advanced, including the deployment of aeroplanes, naval bombardments and, most importantly, British or French Muslim troops. The crucial point, besides ensuring that the revolt did not collapse, was that the French must not appear to have saved it. Bray, fit, keen, and well informed about the region, was chosen to map Rabegh and its environs on the Red Sea Coast. This was undoubtedly risky. On one occasion, Bray dispersed gun-wielding Arabs by rushing towards them, waving his tripod and bellowing abuse. As Bray later recorded in a slightly embellished account of the episode, by virtue of a personal visit to London by him, and a nail-biting intervention at a Cabinet meeting, the British government, amid the many demands on its time and resources, was persuaded that something must be done immediately to support the Arab Revolt.

Bray, having now spent some years analysing and actively countering Muslim unrest, submitted an important memorandum on the Muhammedan Question to the Foreign Office. The paper contained key elements of Bray's intelligence and was also significant in that it chimed with fears being expressed by senior India Office officials especially.

Bray's investigations into the pan-Islamic movement at Jeddah convinced him that Germany and Turkey were intent on using it as a means of destabilising Britain's large Muslim population. In March 1917, he considered it vital to anticipate the actions of 'certain combinations, which may become a potential force and a real danger to us at a later period'. The movement or its seeds encompassed the entire Muslim world, including Persia, Afghanistan, Turkestan, Java, Arabia and the whole Muslim British Empire. His intelligence sources suggested that Russian officials were assisting or actively sympathising with these groups. As Bray continued, pan-Islam must be closely watched. It wasn't simply a matter of 'sincere Mohammedans' wanting independence but 'thousands of . . . fanatics running before they can walk'. Otherwise, unless measures were taken to sever its membranes, it would become 'a real and pressing danger . . . as a weapon in the hands of any future enemy'. Bray advised immediate action on several points. Purely repressive measures would simply drive the organisation underground and Britain would 'lose its threads' or create martyrs. Consequently, Britain must support King Hussein as the best counterweight to subversive Muhammedan movements. If Hussein of Mecca were strengthened in territorial terms, and bolstered by means of military support and propaganda, this would go some way to pricking the bubble of discontent throughout the empire. To Bray, the Arab Revolt was a crusade which had 'nipped in the bud' an attempt to raise Jihad, or holy war, in Arabia, Persia, Afghanistan, and on the North-West Frontier. More broadly, Bray suggested that the grievances of

Muslim Indians must be addressed and that British civil and military officers should be educated about the nature of the problem. He also recommended, in anticipation of a similar War Office proposal of 1919, the centralisation of imperial intelligence gathering, greater circulation of information, and the use of counter-propaganda. Finally, Bray suggested that King Hussein might establish in Mecca a college of religious teaching.

Bray, as witnessed by his gallantry in the field and his special duties in the Hejaz, was, above all, a man of action who sought fulfilment by means of devoted service to King and country. By the end of 1917, Sir Percy Cox, Chief Political Officer with British forces in Mesopotamia, wished to use him and, in March 1918, Bray was posted with only an Egyptian assistant to the 'fanatical' city of Kerbela. There, 'sustained and guarded by the spirit of his country', he proceeded in the best traditions of the 'man on the spot' to defuse a rebellion by 140,000 Arabs. In Bray's words, 'the spirit of England had given peace'. Elsewhere, however, he confessed that his time in Kerbela had been fraught with anxiety. Yet this was understandable. On hearing of the proposed rebellion, Bray acted swiftly. With little time to act, he galloped at top speed to the council chamber of the leading sheikh. Denied even a customary greeting, Bray, realising that he might be killed at any moment, talked with him for several hours and eventually defused the situation. From Kerbela, he was gazetted into the Indian Political Service and posted to Bahrein as British Agent. In this capacity Bray later claimed among other things to have averted a serious breach between the British government and Ibn Saud, for which he was allegedly thanked officially by the Foreign Office.

Bray's employment as a special intelligence officer by the India Office, the crucial period of his career, lasted from August 1920 until approximately the spring of 1923. This position, or rather its title, was apparently unique, certainly within the Foreign or India Offices. Such was the level of concern about worldwide unrest that both offices were desperately anxious to have him, but, after an unseemly row, the India Office prevailed. Until the transfer of Mesopotamian affairs to the Colonial Office, Bray spent most of his time investigating the causes of unrest in that country. Subsequently, he analysed sources of external menace to India, principally Bolshevism. On Bray's appointment John Shuckburgh, head of the Political and Secret Department of the India Office, informed him that he was to investigate the sources of unrest and anti-British activity in Mesopotamia. Crucially, according to Shuckburgh, these sources were felt to be external and it was 'desirable that the whole question should be investigated with as little delay as possible, with a view to tracing the evil to its source'.

Before long Bray had again analysed the 'Asiatic problem', suggesting to the India Office that Britain should create a 'belt of semi-independent States, [from] Aden to Trebizond and from Gaza to the Persian border'. As he continued, 'let Arabia, Kurdistan, Mesopotamia and Armenia govern themselves under our control, let us develop them on similar lines promoting the closest touch with and appreciation of Britain'. In Bray's view this was necessary because of the limitations of aeroplanes and armoured cars, because of the growing threat of nationalism leading to anti-Christian combinations in the east, and because Bray perceived that, whatever repressive measures were taken, the 'Asiatic menace' was likely to grow. Consequently, Britain must unite with the several Arabian factions under her control as a bulwark against it. The reception of Bray's memorandum at the Foreign Office was mixed, but Colin Garbett of the India Office, previously of the civil administrative staff in Mesopotamia, accepted Bray's perception of a conspiracy, observing: 'that there is some common force behind the symptoms we can admit. It may be the machinations of some person or persons; it may be that these symptoms in the East are but manifestations of that intolerance of authority personal, industrial and constitutional which is the characteristic feature of the whole world of today.'

The only known (or suspected) photograph of Childs shows him on a bridge in an atmospheric location, during his journey through Turkey. From *Across Asia Minor on Foot*. (*Blackwood, 1917*)

The indomitable Ely
Bannister Soane, *c*. 1912.
Left, portrait by London
Stereoscopic Co. from
*Through Mesopotamia and
Kurdistan in Disguise*. (*John
Murray, 1912. By kind
permission*)

Below, seated centre, with a
group of Kurds. (*Middle
East Centre, St Antony's
College, Oxford*)

Soane in a group with the Russian consul (*left*). (© *BP Amoco Archive*)

Gateway to the East. A shot of Constantinople (Istanbul) taken around 1915. (*Imperial War Museum*)

Norman Bray in uniform, back row, third from left among a group of Indian Army cavalry officers, the 18th Bengal Lancers, and in close-up below. (*National Army Museum*)

Sinclair, *above* with Eric Lingeman and 'Zobeida', outside the British Consulate at Resht, Persia. *Below*: a spot of duck hunting: Sinclair with guide near Constantinople, *c.* 1919. (*British Library*)

Paul Dukes. Top, portrait by Elliott & Fry, Ltd. reproduced from the *Story of 'ST 25'*. (*Cassell and Company Ltd, 1938*)

Below: Capt A.W.S. Agar VC, DSO, RN (formerly Lt Agar).
Below, right: Dukes in one of his many disguises. (*Brotherton Library*)

Above: Firing breaks out in the Nevsky Prospekt, Petrograd (St Petersburg) in the early days of the Russian revolution, October 1917. (*Imperial War Museum*)

Below: A large gathering of Muslims at prayer in Nigeria during Ramadan. Guided by men like Palmer and Lethem, British policy aimed to prevent a possible Mahdist resurgence. (*The Foreign and Commonwealth Office, London*)

By 1919, the range of difficulties afflicting the British Empire meant that such movements could not be ignored. Officials of the Eastern Department of the Foreign Office were clearly anxious about such conspiracies and efforts were already under way to monitor the activities of potentially unruly elements in England itself. These groups included the Islamic Society, the Egyptian Society in Great Britain, the Islamic Bureau, and the Anglo-Ottoman Society. Bray personally shadowed a delegation from the Khilafat movement whilst it was in England, noting every move of its members in case they made contact with other like-minded parties. He concluded that that movement or organisation hoped to create independent Muslim sovereignty or control throughout the Arab Middle East.

Bray's memoranda, which drew widely upon raw intelligence supplied by SIS officers overseas, seemed to confirm fears of a conspiracy. Much of this intelligence was fragmentary and had to be carefully pieced together by Bray and others. One important exception was an unusually complete report submitted in May 1919 by a Lieutenant Hugh Whittall, formerly on special intelligence service in Switzerland between 1917 and 1918. Whittall had gathered his information from his former agents in Switzerland and from conversations with Young Turks, reformers who had spearheaded the Turkish Revolution of 1908. This information suggested that recent uprisings in India and Egypt had been practise for the ultimate aim of toppling Britain's Muslim empire. Whittall's contacts had convinced him of the existence of a 'close relationship . . . between Germany, the Russian Soviet Republic and the anti-British agitators in the east'. He observed: 'the distinct impression obtained is that a plot is on foot and that its fomenters are only waiting until the conclusion of peace brings further demobilisation and abolishes the present restrictions on international correspondence and traffic to carry it out'.

Like Bray, Whittall noted the key factor of this movement as being the coalescent tendencies of the revolutionaries from many countries who had formerly worked independently. German,

Russian and Turkish money was flooding into Switzerland to support this and the chief perpetrator, according to Whittall, was the German Propaganda Bureau in Berlin. Foreign and India Office officials alike were greatly impressed by Whittall's report. Sir Louis Mallet, formerly British Ambassador in Constantinople, considered it 'remarkable' in that it 'entirely confirms the stray pieces of information which we have been receiving for some time past and it is borne out by what has actually happened and is happening today: in Egypt, Kurdistan, Afghanistan and in Constantinople itself'. Whittall was certainly well suited to the task of gathering this information. A reserve officer of the Royal Navy, seconded to MI1c, a contemporary described him thus: 'He was just under six feet, a dark faced, manly Adonis', who had 'great personality, force of character and courage'. In service with Compton Mackenzie's organisation, he had excelled as an agent in his force of personality, his athleticism and his command of languages.

Bray, Whittall and others sought to counteract these conspiracies by means of equally broad-ranging intelligence gathering or counter-propaganda. In 1919, a centralised postwar intelligence-gathering structure in the Middle East was being discussed. The idea was the brainchild of Brigadier-General Deedes on the staff of General Milne at Constantinople. Briefly, the plan envisaged the establishing of intelligence contacts or of intelligence-gathering centres, offshoots of the British Arab Bureau in Cairo relocated in Constantinople, in a great swathe of countries from Singapore, through Central Asia, the Arabian Peninsula, Somaliland, East and North Africa, Spain, Gibraltar, Malta and the Balkans, and encompassing the existing intelligence network in Switzerland. For some time the Arab Bureau had assessed intelligence obtained in a broad geographical area including, in the context of pan-Islamism, East Central Africa and the East Indies.

Bray became an important figure, proselytising on the pan-Islamic threat, and, more broadly, on the connections between it

116

and a general 'pan-Orientalism' which, by 1920, he perceived to be sweeping across the entire eastern world. Bray included in this the whole of North Africa and, in so far as his information went, the whole of Asia, less China. Some Foreign Office officials had reservations about Bray's judgement, but his continued involvement in the analysis of the emerging eastern unrest was deemed important; chiefly because, unlike any of his contemporaries, he gave some definition to what remained a nebulous and shadowy concept. This was true with reference both to specific outbreaks, as in Mesopotamia, and to the broader picture of events in a vast arc of territory stretching from Morocco to Aden and from Switzerland to Japan.

Fears of such broad-based conspiracies were also reflected in some press coverage of Britain's imperial difficulties. In several articles published in July 1920 in the *Morning Post* under the title 'The Cause of World Unrest', it was argued that, 'there has long existed, like a canker at the heart of our civilization, a secret revolutionary sect, mainly of Judaic origin, bent on the destruction of all Christian Empires, altars and thrones'. The authors attributed the revolutions in Turkey, Russia and Germany to the existence of Masonic movements hijacked by a small number of revolutionary Jewish elements. Their activities, as an external element exploiting internal tensions, stemmed from similarly broad networks of secret societies in pre-revolutionary France. In 1920, the tentacles of this movement were allegedly inspiring labour unrest in Britain and fomenting all aspects of imperial rebellion in the empire.

In an attempt to put flesh on the bones of eastern unrest late in 1920, Bray submitted a memorandum to the India Office on 'Events in Asia'. In his view a relatively new strain of 'Asiatic thought' had emerged. It was influenced chiefly by American republicanism and by German militarism and its manifestations as a religious phenomenon belied the fact that it was chiefly a 'weapon of political value'. The worrying factor was that, sustained as it was by vigorous propaganda, it was a progressive

117

movement gradually undermining sympathy for Britain in Asia. At times of crisis, Bray felt, these hostile elements might coalesce. Already it had taken 'firm and unshakeable hold on the minds of Orientals' and repressive measures would simply fan the flames of discontent. What Britain had chiefly to fear, he warned, was not the isolated action of one such Asiatic state but its coalition with an enemy of Britain – probably Russia – in the event of future hostilities. Bray also feared unrest developing into 'concerted rebellion' in the Dominions, assisted by neighbouring Asiatic states. The difficulty, as Bray noted, was that if Asiatic nations did in the future attain advanced development or freedom from British control, there was a risk that they might attribute this not to British beneficence but to the success of violent agitation. Having identified the nature of the problem, Bray offered a solution. Essentially Britain must coordinate her intelligence machinery in the east and she must also rally pro-British elements to her defence.

According to Bray, the content, style and dissemination patterns of press, newspapers, pamphlets and books throughout the Middle East and Central Asia appeared to confirm his view that there were several key propaganda centres. Each had a radius, and tracking the movements of its agents could plot its extent. The activities of these individuals were wide-ranging: minor incidents and issues, especially those with a religious dimension, were distorted; individual grudges were nurtured, and inspirational teachers of religion and other divines were sworn to the cause. They, in turn, disseminated anti-British feelings among their pupils. These Talabas were usually young men of 'quick intelligence and active bodies' who became utterly devoted and subservient so that, in the case of one teacher of Bray's acquaintance, he had over 200 disciples. Religious and secular societies, including the Freemasons, were also used. Unless Britain acted quickly the future was bleak. Children throughout the Middle East were being taught to 'despise the Christian peoples'. Bray also offered evidence of the practical methods whereby enemy agents infiltrated information to contacts in areas or towns controlled by Britain, and claimed to have reasonably precise examples of this in an area stretching from Switzerland through Mecca to India.

Bray's memorandum tied in precisely with the anxieties of the British Cabinet. In the previous month the Foreign Secretary, Lord Curzon, had informed his Cabinet colleagues that the Soviet government was completely unable to adhere to 'correct international behaviour'. According to Curzon, its agents had for long been intriguing in Britain and overseas 'to overthrow our institutions everywhere and to destroy our prestige and authority, particularly in Asia'. Simply stated, the Bolsheviks aimed to subvert and destroy Britain's connection with the Indian Empire.

As to the unrest in Mesopotamia, Bray traced it to external sources. Unlike some officials, he did not regard its origins as lying solely in 'local discontent or [in a] fault in administration'. Nor did he regard any political group or section of the population as being solely responsible. However, according to his information, the educated classes were the conduit for hostile external forces. According to Bray, their powerful commitment to independence might easily be turned to violent action in order to achieve it. These elements had allied with pro-Turkish Iraqis by virtue of propaganda engineered from outside, principally by Turkish nationalists who, in turn, looked to Germany and Russia for support. The assumption was that all of these forces could unite on the basis of pan-Islamic aims, with the ultimate goal of removing British and French influence from the Middle East. Besides the active involvement of the principal Turkish nationalist and Arab leaders, including Mustafa Kemal and Prince Feisal, Bray argued that much of the preparatory work had been undertaken by secret societies. The most important of these were, in Anatolia and Syria respectively, Mouvahiddin and Nadi-al Arabi. The activities of both societies had been traced to Switzerland and thence to Berlin, and the Nadi-al Arabi also controlled or had direct links with the Al Ahd movement in Mesopotamia and with nationalists there.

The spectre at the feast in all of this was the Soviet regime. Bray was convinced that its ultimate aim, as a means of attaining worldwide loyalty to communism, was the destruction of British power in the east. The principal tool in realising this scheme was to induce indigenous revolt. British agents were discovering intensive propaganda efforts among secret societies with roots in urban and rural areas. In geopolitical terms, Bray felt that Britain could do little to forestall this influence. Hostility towards Bolshevism in Anatolia and in Afghanistan was overshadowed by the prevalence of the creed in Persia and Armenia. Russia, 'the enemy of civilization', according to Bray, was teaching the 'Eastern world new lessons in statecraft and intrigue'. A combination of consular representatives, military occupation and political missions had enabled Moscow to extend her 'sinister tentacles' and exploit and convert to her cause, discontented elements throughout the Middle East and Central Asia.

Germany, with whom Moscow had a 'clear and close understanding', assisted by Enver and Talaat, leading figures in the Committee of Union and Progress (CUP), had forged a working agreement with Berlin, Moscow, and pan-Arabs.* This, in turn, was based upon an 'Asiatic Islamic Federation', which drew its strength from the dissatisfaction of Turkish and Syrian nationalists and from pan-Arabs in Syria. According to Bray, it was only with the creation of this Federation that Germany and Russia were prepared to support Enver's expansionist aims in the Caucasus. The Federation was extended to include a defensive alliance with Feisal, King Hussein's son, at a secret meeting in Montreux in November 1919. Further intelligence suggested that other potentially hostile groups were being courted. In fact, Bray detected 'the inception of a general strategic plan directed ostensibly from Moscow, against France and England'.

---

* Enver and Talaat were, with Jamal Pasha, key figures in the Young Turk Movement and had seized power in 1913.

In the following months, Bray produced several memoranda about wide-ranging conspiracies against the British Empire. In his view, these forces were at work in the Middle East – but sections of the British press that opposed an active British military response to the Soviet threat were also being subsidised by Moscow. Every effort had to be made to split these forces or to provide the Turkish government with the means of undermining the nationalists. Bray suggested briefing Arab leaders on the true nature of the Soviet threat and the necessity of greater cooperation between Britain and France on intelligence matters. Similarly, he deemed vital an improved coordination of existing British intelligence agencies in the Middle East and the creation of a special service of counter-espionage officers with specialist skills. He also recommended decisive action against Al Ahd and counter-propaganda in Central Asia and Trans-Caucasia. Directly anticipating measures introduced by Edwin Montagu, Secretary of State for India, Bray also proposed an interdepartmental committee or meetings to consider the issue. Far from dismissing this as fantastic, as did other departments, Major-General Thwaites, Director of Military Operations and Intelligence, considered Bray's analysis to be 'moderate' and that it 'confirm[ed] our own views'.

Intercepted messages from Suritz, the Bolshevik envoy in Kabul, to the Bolshevik Bureaux of Foreign Affairs in Moscow and Tashkent, suggested to Bray that Soviet propagandists had already penetrated India. In Bray's opinion these reports offered conclusive proof of Bolshevik attempts to establish a 'Soviet India' as an element in their 'wider web embracing the East from Egypt to China'. In pursuit of this, the Bolsheviks had already established links with centres of unrest and propaganda in India. Afghanistan was a cat's paw in this, and was also instrumental in inducing unrest across India's frontier. Bray's proposed solution was straightforward: as a precursor to a proposed Anglo-Soviet commercial agreement, the Russo-Afghan connection should be severed, principally by the cancellation of their treaty. Bray further specified that no Russian consulates or other agencies were to be established on Afghan territory, that Russia was not to import arms or ammunition there, that she was to withdraw subsidies, to cease anti-British propaganda there, in Chinese Turkestan and on the north-eastern frontier. Russia was also to stop exporting anti-British literature, to stop intriguing among frontier tribes, and was to accept the closure of the instructional centre at Tashkent and a prohibition on the establishing of similar bodies elsewhere.

In Bray's view, the Bolsheviks, the CUP and the Turkish nationalists were also harnessed in an alliance, principally one of convenience, which aimed to defeat the British Empire. Evidence suggested that Talaat and his associates aimed to reconstitute the Turkish Empire by absorbing Azerbaijan, Georgia and Turkestan. The 'stumbling block' in this was the British Empire and, accordingly, the CUP sought to exploit Anglo-Russian hostility. Bray argued that Talaat had worked tirelessly to create an understanding with the Arab movement and with Egyptian and Indian nationalists and between those elements and Russia. The Soviet leadership supported nationalist sentiments in various countries throughout Asia to gain allies and to exploit Islam against the British Empire in a manner that would not backfire. If the Bolshevik leadership did not contemplate a direct onslaught on Britain's position in India, Bray found the continued increase of her military forces in the Caucasus and Central Asia worrying and difficult to explain. To facilitate Soviet military objectives and to prevent Turkish imperial ambitions, Armenia had been effectively Sovietised. In Bray's opinion, without measures to bolster Mustafa Kemal there was a 'grave danger of complete Bolshevik control' in Turkey.

Bray's thoughts on the outbreaks in Mesopotamia and other aspects of anti-British conspiracies caused alarm at the India Office. The Government of India had instituted various measures to deal with unrest and conspiratorial movements in India itself. These had included the interception of Russian wireless messages, counter-propaganda, border controls, intelligence gathering, legislation, port control, and the formation of the Special Bureau of Information. By the autumn of 1920 an impression had grown at the India Office that this was not enough and that the Government of India was attributing a rash of strikes to local factors when the true source was external. It was amid mounting anxieties of this kind that Bray was asked to investigate in more detail the nature of the Bolshevik threat to India.

In his memorandum on 'Bolshevism in India', Bray alerted his superiors to the scope and nature of the Bolshevik threat to India, that keystone of the British Empire. (Some might argue that there was mutual dependance between Britain and India.) The limited available intelligence regarding links between the Bolsheviks and Indian extremists indicated that communications did exist and that propaganda efforts if confronted would not cease but simply become more circumspect. An additional and increasing threat would be felt in colonial possessions as the Bolsheviks attempted to boost their moral strength in contradiction of the spirit of the Anglo-Russian Trade Agreement. By virtue of that accord, Britain and Russia had agreed to cease propaganda and other hostile activities. In practical terms, a network of routes for hostile influence converged on India from Egypt, Mesopotamia, Java, the North-West Frontier, Burma and Singapore. Bray's information seemed to confirm fears that the government of India was ducking the issue. Furthermore, as Bray had pointed out, Bolshevik efforts to set India ablaze did not necessarily require the personal physical presence of Bolshevik agents. As Hirtzel noted, wherever they were, they could be relied upon to 'make the agitators' pot boil'.

In the first months of 1921, Bray extended his horizons. Drawing on his experience in the field, besides papers on the Bolshevik threat, he also examined the Khilafat Movement, similar movements in the Dutch East Indies, and the activities of Egyptian nationalists. According to Bray, it was essential to assess the relative importance of these elements with regard to the internal situation in Britain's eastern empire and in India itself. In his spare moments, Bray also attended interdepartmental committees as an expert on behalf of the India Office. The first of these, which met on four occasions early in 1921, examined the means of safeguarding British interests in the east and subsequently analysed the political considerations of the Soviet government. Bray's contributions to this body, and his memorandum on 'Bolshevik Intrigue' circulated to the Cabinet by Montagu in June 1921, pointed to the need for more formalised correlation and assessment of intelligence on eastern movements. Bray did not argue that Soviet Russia was an immediate *military* threat, but he did not preclude it becoming so. He argued that Soviet activities had 'created a situation actually dangerous to the British Empire'. Montagu and Hirtzel agreed, and in June 1921, amid press reports of the 'Red Menace' and such-like, Montagu contacted several key departments to suggest the formation of an interdepartmental committee to examine the problem in greater detail.

Bray's involvement in the activities of the highly secret Interdepartmental Committee on Bolshevism as a Menace to the British Empire was significant, if brief. The Foreign Office, having shelved its previous reservations about his judgement, now approached the issue of imperial conspiracies with urgency. Curzon was keen that Bray should continue to gather evidence of Soviet intrigues so that he might challenge their government. The reports of that body and of its successor, the Interdepartmental Committee on Eastern Unrest, presented a detailed overview of the several threats confronting the British Empire. Its analysis, dating from August 1922, was based largely upon a perception of a prevalent 'spirit of restlessness' that Bray had analysed in detail over the previous two years. Bray's involvement in the preparation of these reports was clear from the expansive scope and style of its analysis. The collapse of the Russian Empire, economic hardship, the spreading of arms to eastern countries, and Wilsonian idealism were all factors in this emerging danger.

Bray and others like him clearly felt that these terroristic elements were not isolated from each other. In particular, pan-

Islamic propaganda had 'resulted in a close sympathy between the different Mohammedan States'. The focus of the unrest was India, where Bolshevik penetration was proceeding through several channels, including Afghanistan, Persia, Tashkent, and the Pamirs. In Persia and Afghanistan the Soviets were supporting existing Bolshevik or pan-Islamic elements. Bolshevism was being spread by propaganda training schools, and by encouragement to frontier tribes hostile to Britain. According to the report, Soviet arms and money were being infiltrated to the North-West Frontier from Afghanistan, whose amir was generally receptive to anti-British feelings. Turkish nationalist intrigue was filtering towards India via Syria, Mesopotamia, Persia and Afghanistan under the guise of anti-imperialist bodies and, more importantly, pan-Islamic organs. Some of these were supported unofficially by Britain's rivals such as France, Germany and Italy. Indian students and revolutionaries were also being lured into anti-British or anti-European activities and had established centres of resistance in America, Japan, Central Asia, Afghanistan, and in several European capitals including Moscow.

Bray's involvement in analysing eastern unrest culminated in the establishing of the Interdepartmental Committee on Eastern Unrest and an urgent late-night summons from Lord Curzon, the Foreign Secretary, in May 1923. Then, both men worked into the night to draft a note of protest to the Soviet government. Bray's resignation from the India Office and from the government of India soon afterwards – and shortly after receiving an OBE for his work in combating unrest – was not the end of his official connections, although several government departments would come to wish otherwise. As Bray grappled with world unrest, his wife battled less successfully with personal demons and was on the brink of insanity. On the advice of the foremost alienists of the day, he was told to move his family abroad to seek a cure.

Unable to return to India because of his young family, Bray found employment as a Passport Control Officer in Copenhagen where, it seems he may have replaced the mysterious L.G.M.

Gall, who had apparently been working for SIS under cover of a post with the British Legation. Both in Copenhagen and in Geneva, where he next worked as Passport Control Officer, Bray was almost certainly an agent of SIS. In Geneva, Bray used his extensive intelligence contacts to thwart plans for a revolution in Egypt hatched by the former Khedive. During this episode he was betrayed and then arrested by the German authorities but, in moments of critical danger, escaped by swallowing the information. Later, he was forced to dodge bullets in Lausanne when he became the target of frustrated terrorists.

Clearly, these activities indicated a more active rôle than that of one assigned to monitor passports and would-be immigrants. The use of the Passport Control Office as a 'fine-meshed sieve' to vet visa applicants and as a means of monitoring the movement of international revolutionaries, was well established by the 1920s. Bray, as a young, fit, linguistically gifted officer with a taste for adventure and a broad knowledge of revolutionary movements, would have been a natural choice for the service. He had most probably made contact with SIS in 1920; by 1922, there was strong opposition from Special Branch, from Director of Intelligence Sir Basil Thomson, and from SIS itself to the proposed scaling down of the passport service. Such a move would greatly increase the expenditure of SIS on its overseas operations and would also help Bolshevik and nationalist intrigues. As to Bray's selection for a post in Switzerland, Sir Wyndham Childs, Assistant Commissioner of the Metropolitan Police, noted that the country was a 'nest of Turkish-cum-Bulgarian-cum-Indian intrigue, all directed towards the "liberation" of so-called oppressed nationalities, including India, Egypt and Irak, and all modelling themselves on Ireland for this purpose'.

Quite when Bray left SIS is unclear. According to his own account, his services were dispensed with because he had found himself to be temperamentally unsuited to the work. Returning to England, Bray was appointed Secretary of the Junior Carlton

Club, a position that was not, perhaps, too distant from the world of espionage. Then, as a soapbox orator across England and as a political campaigner for the Conservative Party, Bray detected 'an apathy for the Imperial destiny . . . [that] cover[ed] the Nation as a cloud'. Hoping to instil greater patriotism in his country, Bray also clearly aspired to a more active and influential position in the great events that were shaping. Although a senior position eluded him in the remainder of his lifetime, he certainly gained a degree of notoriety with his former employers.

Just prior to his resignation from the Junior Carlton Club, Bray was introduced to Dr Thorst, Adolf Hitler's 'representative' in England. Bray subsequently found himself a mediator for a Dr Rosenburg, Hitler's emissary, who met with Lord Hailsham, Secretary for War, and Lord Exeter in order to deliver 'an important message' from Hitler. After consulting Hailsham and other members of the club, Bray subsequently accepted an invitation from Rosenburg to meet Hitler personally in Berlin 'as he had a proposition of most vital importance to both our countries'.* Having apparently disagreed strongly over the question of Danzig, and sternly rebutted Hitler's accusations of Foreign Office interference, Bray recalled:

I asked Hitler what his intentions were regarding the Jewish minority. He assured me that, beyond his intentions to extradite a number to their own country since a lot of Jews had infiltrated into Germany during the last war to the detriment of German citizens, he had no animus against the Jews and would not molest them. I said 'That is well, my countrymen do not like the ill-treatment of minorities.' I also informed him that his so-called 'representative' in this country was a menace.

* Unfortunately, the late Lord Hailsham ignored my request to research this episode among the papers left by his father. Lord Exeter's appointment diaries, which are now held at Northamptonshire Record Office, indicate his involvement with the Junior Carlton Club but, as might be expected if he were in regular contact with its secretary, there is no mention of that individual by name.

At a further meeting with Rosenberg and Prince Bismarck in Claridges Hotel, Bray stated that, on account of the ill-treatment of the Jews, he now had no wish for further contact with Rosenberg. Before this meeting, Bray recalled that he had received a visit from the head of SIS, Sir Hugh Sinclair, who had shown him an inaccurate record of his journey to Germany and had warned him against any further undertakings of this kind. We now know that there were many contacts between British and German politicians and leaders at this time and we also know, from files released to the PRO, that British intelligence officers were sent to Germany to discover Hitler's intentions. In fact, it seems that Sinclair may have warned Bray off because of a mission undertaken to Germany in 1933 by Captain G.M. Liddell on behalf of the Security Service and SIS, the details of which can now be read at the PRO. Liddell apparently went to Germany at the invitation of the Nazis to examine material that had been gathered by the German political police, concerning movements and groups hostile to Britain. Some of the material related to Indian seditionists and the Anti-Imperial League.

By 1936, Bray had moved to Majorca, where he started a commissioned autobiography. There, feeling that another World War was imminent, he studied the developing Spanish civil war and gathered information for the Admiralty and the Air Ministry on an informal basis. His subsequent return to England was eventful. Whilst in Spain his publisher had sold out and the vendor had gone bankrupt. Penniless, Bray borrowed money and wrote a cheque which was later returned. This led to a complaint against him by the Foreign Office whilst he was literally starving on the streets of Marseilles.

In 1943, Bray, evidently itching for a more active rôle in the war, complained that his desire to be employed in the Middle East had been thwarted by charges made against him by the Foreign and War Offices. On investigation by the Air Ministry it seems that a section of military intelligence at the War Office had blocked his request because his name had arisen in connection with investigations into suspicious contacts with Germany prior to the war. This complaint and further charges of fascist sympathies had been levelled against Bray, something that he rejected as 'fantastic and utterly devoid of truth'. In his defence, besides mounting a highly emotional appeal to his sovereign, Bray repeatedly suggested that he had gone to Germany at the instance of Lord Hailsham and, moreover, that he had been asked to apply for further employment on intelligence duties. Bray felt that his complaint had been deliberately obstructed, when he had 'sacrificed so much, risked so much and suffered so much' for his country.

Whatever the truth of Bray's life – and there must remain a question mark over some matters of varying importance – his influence as an intelligence gatherer and analyst of hostile movements in Asia cannot be doubted. In accepting views about the coalescent tendencies of Britain's enemies, British officials, Bray included, were conceptually unable to understand those movements and their often incompatible aims. In assessing these threats, Bray was not irresponsible. On the contrary, if he had lived today, his skills might have been put to excellent use in the pursuit and apprehension of international terrorists and in understanding their modus operandi. If his views were unpalatable to some colleagues, then it must be remembered that Foreign and India Office officials and SIS officers had expressed fears of broad-based conspiracies before Bray took up employment there and set down his thoughts in commissioned memoranda. Curzon was also prey to such fears for the duration of his foreign secretaryship, as indeed was Edwin Montagu at the India Office. Bray's importance to senior politicians in the aftermath of war would suggest that there was, perhaps, considerably more to him than the 'well-intentioned', 'honourable' officer with a persecution complex, once described by T.E. Lawrence.*

---

* T.E. Shaw (Lawrence) to C.F. Shaw, 23 November 1934, Add. Ms 45904, British Library.

How to spend a cheap holiday on the continent (*W.K. Haselden*, Daily Mirror, *1912*)

5

Wanderings of the 'Moneyed Tramp'

TURKISH AFFAIRS AND THE BAGHDAD RAILWAY

On a particularly cold and stormy day in October 1911, a solitary figure might have been observed disembarking from an Austrian coal-steamer at the Black Sea port of Samsun. After an overnight stay, over the next five months the traveller proceeded on foot to Alexandretta on the Mediterranean coast. However, during a journey of almost 1,300 miles, this mysterious traveller spent only fifty-four days on the road.

The identity of William John Childs can first be traced with any degree of certainty to a passport application in the spring of 1910. Quite why, at the age of 42, he chose to undertake this adventure may never be entirely clear. Indeed, much of his life prior to this remains a mystery. In the autumn of 1911, having apparently been delayed unavoidably in Constantinople, he embarked upon a journey which he recorded in his book, *Across Asia Minor on Foot*, first published in 1917 by W. Blackwood & Sons. Further excerpts, relating various travels in Asia Minor, followed in *Blackwood's Magazine* and in the *Journal of the Royal Central Asian Society* between 1915 and 1916.

From these and other sources, we know that Childs was no stranger to travel in Asia Minor. He had, it seems, previously spent a year at Samsun, probably using it as a base for forays into the interior. Childs had also possibly travelled in France, Greece, the Balkans, Germany, Italy, Norway and Australia. By 1912, if not earlier, he was resident in Constantinople, where he lived in total for two years, witnessing and recording the arrival in that year of the *Goeben*, the infamous German battleship. We also know that Childs had an extremely inquisitive mind; that he was gifted in the breadth of his interests, particularly in his knowledge of the classical past of Asia Minor; that he was something of an amateur archaeologist, architectural historian and numismatist; that, whatever his past, he was by his own admission, no stranger to the sight of blood.

Childs readily admitted that his book contained 'no bloodletting [and] no hair-breadth escapes'. Yet it did contain a fascinating picture of a region of extreme diversity in race, politics, history, economy, art and culture. Childs was supremely fitted to record this. A disciplined diarist, he was in no hurry to traverse the region. He was, if we are to believe scarce autobiographical references, 'a civilian traveller', 'a moneyed tramp', who had no particular itinerary or official brief. This author has found no conclusive evidence to the contrary. A discovery of references among collections of private papers to an officer by the name of Childs working at the War Office, periodically in an intelligence capacity prior to and during the Great War, were intriguing but ultimately disappointing. That Childs, Wyndham (later Sir Wyndham) Childs, who was also a captain at the time, was appointed to the War Office to head a section which would deal with atrocities and breaches of international law.

Yet, of course, the evolution of military intelligence prior to 1914 was such that William Childs would not have left any discernible trail even for the most determined historian. Instructions issued in 1909 to officers undertaking intelligence-gathering duties overseas, were emphatic that in official communications they should be absolutely silent regarding their true purposes. Furthermore, the officer 'should understand that he ha[d] no official mission for the Director of Military Operations, but can only be considered as travelling on his private affairs'. Would-be intelligence officers were to be briefed on native laws regarding foreign espionage in their country of travel, no incriminating papers were to be carried and, in general, payment could only be expected for results obtained.

Yet, by the autumn of 1917, if not earlier, Childs had turned his experience to official purposes. In a wartime intelligence department, he was ideally suited to contribute his knowledge to the preparation of detailed information for the benefit of Britain's peacemakers. Prior to this, although his exact official position cannot now be confirmed, Childs may have discovered a suitable niche working for Military Intelligence. His manner was unobtrusive, he was a silent and meticulous chronicler, an observer of people, customs and events, enjoying the odd moment of passionate involvement in his narrative; sufficient at least to alert the reader to the possibility that his travels may not have gone entirely unnoticed by officials in Whitehall and Constantinople.

* * *

The ambiguities surrounding Childs's employment in that city prior to and after his journey are not helped by the immense diversity of life in Constantinople at that time. An examination of contemporary Foreign Office Embassy correspondence registers, reveals a rich variety of individuals and organisations with interests in the city or in the Turkish interior. Commercial and industrial agents, educators, bankers, post-office officials, journalists, servicemen attached to the Turkish Army, and even travellers with aliases bound for the interior all played a part. More remote parts of the region were gradually being accessed by British industry and commerce and the size of the British community likewise ensured an extremely diverse retinue. There was also the large embassy staff, fleeting glimpses of clerks, lawyers, archivists, commercial staff, librarians, military attachés, and, perhaps, of other less reputable figures employed by Fitzmaurice, the highly regarded dragoman at the embassy, who, by the time of Childs's arrival in Turkey, channelled Secret Service funds in the region.

By 1911, when Childs embarked on his journey, the British government had for some time been keenly aware of growing international rivalries in Asia Minor. The policies of Disraeli and Salisbury from the 1870s had pointed to a more energetic involvement in the region, with Scanderoon or Alexandretta, as it came to be known, identified as a vital port for launching a counter-offensive against a Russian advance on India. As Childs later recalled during his journey and his residence in Constantinople, there was no mistaking the identity of Britain's 'traditional enemy'. In the previous half-century, Russia's massive territorial gains had produced decades of tension, friction and, occasionally, the prospect of war. The 1907 Anglo-Russian Agreement did little to dim memories of this period, particularly among those who had studied at first hand the territory between the vast empires of Russia and Great Britain. Childs, for one, considered it inevitable that Russia would one day possess Samsun, 'the southern Odessa of the Black Sea'. It was this lingering and sinister threat that Childs perceived at the outset of his journey when he detected 'a sense of mystery and possible adventure . . . where someone lurked who had his reasons for wishing to remain unseen'.

Though some came to doubt the efficacy of attempting to defend India at or near Alexandretta, early in the new century German influence at Constantinople began to cause alarm in London. In particular, there was the Berlin–Baghdad Railway, with proposed termini on the Persian Gulf and at Alexandretta. Besides any strategic factors, if Britain ceded control of either port, the largely unexploited trade of the intervening region, the fabled 'Garden of Eden' would be lost to her. To counter this, as a means of maintaining British prestige and interests in international concession hunting in the region, a number of Military Vice-Consuls were appointed to various posts in Asia Minor. The Military Operations Directorate of the War Office was only too glad to volunteer young officers, skilled in languages and topography, who might also preserve the status quo among warring factions, in a region frequently plunged into racial violence.

Childs was acutely sensitive to incipient racial tensions in Asia Minor, noting in his book the 'ever-listening ear and watchful eye for sounds and signs' among a population inured to 'blind fanatical and racial fury'. His path traversed many areas in which racial massacres had occurred and he spent several weeks on the Cilician Plain, much of it in or around Adana, the scene of particularly serious outbreaks in 1909. Childs's examination of the underlying tensions between Armenians, Arabs, Greeks, Turks and Kurds, led him to attribute, as causes of the 1909 massacre, religious, racial, economic, political and local factors. Typically, his generation had much sympathy for the Armenian race; rather less, perhaps, for the Turks. Childs himself found Armenians industrious and warlike but, as a nation, fatally compromised by their 'faculty for dissension'. During the First World War, this balance of sympathies, particularly as between Armenian and Kurd, was modified. Pledges of support for the Armenians from senior politicians could not easily be forgotten. Important debates about British Middle Eastern strategy inevitably highlighted the Armenian nation as a potentially useful tool in promoting British interests in the region. Yet there was also a growing awareness of similar atrocities perpetrated by Armenians on their enemies and, indeed, of the warlike capabilities of the Kurds – a nation that Childs found impossible to admire. As to the Greek population of Asia Minor, Childs found them manipulative, materialistic, and, briefly, fallen from a greatness to which he was romantically drawn.

In the Turkish officer class, Childs discerned 'undeveloped sporting instincts'; a damning charge from one such as Childs, yet the soldiery was apparently more worthy. With British officers, Childs maintained, they 'would be troops of another sort, wanting nothing in dash and nothing in stubbornness'.

The result of the interest shown by Disraeli and Salisbury in the region was that, for a number of years between 1879 and 1882, and again from the mid-1890s, a steady stream of intelligence, not always satisfactory, found its way from Van, Sivas, Mersina,

Adana, and other far-flung outposts onto the desks of civil servants and ministers in London. In particular, the War Office was always desperately anxious for current information on railway projects and, more especially, on the potentialities of the Alexandretta region. In 1905–6, Lt Col Maunsell, Britain's Military Attaché in Constantinople, with Captain Mark Sykes and the Hon George Lloyd, Honorary Attachés there, provided detailed reports and mapping of various regions of Asia Minor, northern Syria and Mesopotamia. Of particular interest to their superiors was the progress of the Baghdad Railway, the vehicle of Germany's *Drang nach Osten*, or drive to the east. By 1910, Military Consuls had dwindled to a few. In the same year, the legendary Commercial Attaché in Constantinople, Ernest Weakley, traversed the region producing, on behalf of the Intelligence Committee of the Board of Trade, a detailed report on the economic potential of Syria and the Alexandretta basin.

Yet the War Office craved political and military intelligence and, in the early part of 1911, revived the scheme of Military Consuls with the despatch to Adana of a lieutenant of the Somerset Light Infantry. The various appointments to this and nearby consular posts in the period 1910 to 1913 have been difficult to follow with precision; partly, it seems, because of a fairly rapid turnover of consular officials. Whilst the adventure offered by postings to exotic eastern locations undoubtedly appealed to young entrants into the Levant Consular Service, surviving correspondence with the Foreign Office reveals that disease, harsh living conditions and dissatisfaction with pay were not uncommon. The Foreign Office was often inflexible in its treatment of these officials, denying them, for instance, the opportunity to submit articles to magazines based upon their experiences. As far as Military Vice-Consuls were concerned, there was the fear that their military careers would be disadvantaged by their secondment. That Childs was a member of the Levant Consular Service or even a commissioned Army officer who served as a Military Consul remains a possibility, although his name has not appeared in this context in copies of the *Army List* or in any Foreign Office, Treasury or other document examined by this author. Certainly, the area he later felt most comfortable dealing with when undertaking official research work, corresponded with the geographical remit of the Levant Service; and he shared the indifferent command of the Turkish language demonstrated by some candidates for the consular examinations at this time. The fact that Childs spent a year at Samsun at some point prior to embarking upon his journey is interesting but inconclusive. British firms were involved in port construction on the Black Sea coast and there was still a Consular Agency in Samsun as late as July 1911.

Thus, in the years prior to the First World War, the War Office was generally keen to continue intelligence-gathering activities in Asia Minor. In March 1902, the Director General of Mobilisation and Military Intelligence had suggested that Captain Tyrrell, the newly appointed Military Vice-Consul at Van, might travel to his post via Alexandretta and Diarbekir as information on those areas was much needed. Two years later, partly with a view to reinforcing British interests in railway concessions in the region, a Captain Smyth surveyed the railway route Mersina–Adana–Killis–Aleppo, much of it later to be traversed by Childs. In November 1910, William Tyrrell, Assistant Under-Secretary at the Foreign Office, suggested to Sir Gerard Lowther, Britain's Ambassador in Constantinople, that the Adana Consulate should be turned into a Military Vice-Consulate on a temporary basis to permit an Army officer to gather information around Alexandretta. The matter was 'somewhat pressing', especially as the situation following the Armenian massacres of 1909 had prevented a similar posting at that time. As Tyrrell concluded, he had already obtained the sanction of the Treasury to the proposal. In any case, Lieutenant Smith was placed at the disposal of the Foreign Office in February 1911 and he remained at Adana until November. An official of the Levant Service, Monck Mason, then replaced him, temporarily, until Shipley, then Consul at Philippopolis, could be relieved. This move was deemed necessary because of the unsettled conditions caused by the Italo-Turkish War. It was amid these currents that the seemingly innocuous, pipe-smoking Childs, encumbered with tins of butter, Cambridge sausages, bacon rashers – in fact, with the makings of an 'honest English breakfast' for each day of his journey – commenced his wanderings in Asia Minor.

Back in London, early in 1915, Childs observed of his writing that it was 'the trivial in its proper place' that gave it reality. It was intended as travel writing and aimed to develop the features of the region, human, social, racial and others. The reality also emerged from the unobtrusive nature of the narrator, providing an occasional glimpse of self-observation. Though conservative in his culinary tastes, an eccentric character emerges, a straw-hatted historian, capable of devouring gargantuan breakfasts, a foreigner with only a smattering of Turkish in the interior of Asia Minor; in which area it was said, 'anything can happen'.

Yet Childs was anything but eccentric in his powers of observation. The attributes of the four Muslims who accompanied him at various stages of his journey were subjected to minute analysis; likewise, an apparently unsuspecting German Consul, charged with the direction of building work on the Baghdad Railway. As the Consul talked freely and continued working in his office, Childs, reclining in a chair, pipe in hand, scrutinised him closely. So, also, the eager British Consul from Adana, who accompanied Childs for several days. Coincidence, perhaps, that consular duties led him to inspect the area at precisely the same time as Childs. Coincidence, or indeed misfortune, that of the area of greatest interest to Britain – the Alexandretta basin – Childs, equipped with two cameras, apparently retrieved no photographs from a film which did not develop.

By the end of 1914, Childs had discussed with the publisher, G.W. Blackwood, the idea of submitting articles on his experiences in Turkey to *Blackwood's Magazine*. Early in 1915, Childs secured from Blackwood the right to use the material in his articles in a manuscript for his book, *Across Asia Minor on Foot*. Blackwood was interested in publishing the book as well as the articles and accepted Childs's request that he receive royalties on the book and an advance on these on delivery of the manuscript. As Childs confessed 'after three years of war in Turkey [he had] acquired some of the qualities of a refugee', and over the next few years he had several temporary addresses, all of them, with one exception, in Surrey.* At this stage, Childs predicted the need for a further three months to complete the book to his 'tolerable satisfaction'. He was, in any case, then apparently not obliged to undertake war work of any kind, informing Blackwood that he was able to devote his whole time to the project. Other aspects of his research and of his life as a writer emerge from the correspondence with Blackwood.

Writing on 30 April, Childs recalled that in the two years he had spent at Constantinople 'in which I rambled much in out of the way nooks and corners, and along both sides of the Bosphorus I acquired a good deal of matter. For my amusement and not for publication, I wrote a few short sketches embodying what I saw.' Whilst Childs did not then consider them suitable for *Blackwood's Magazine* or *'Maga'* as he called it, he felt that if reworked they might provide an interesting article to coincide with the predicted fall of Constantinople to British arms 'in a month or six weeks'. The nature of his occupation whilst at Constantinople remains unclear; yet, as he pointed out in connection with an article entitled 'An Aegean Voyage', he had clearly made several journeys and sojourns along the Aegean coastline, in Thrace and in the interior of Asia Minor. Childs's success in having no fewer than six pieces published in successive issues of *'Maga'*, was a fine achievement in his reckoning; and the degree of his enthusiasm, apart from any other evidence, suggests that, prior to his stay in Constantinople, he had not made his living from writing.

---

* None of their current occupants have been able to supply me with further information.

In the summer of 1915, Childs was mainly preoccupied with writing – yet the completion and delivery of his book was repeatedly delayed. At the end of November, he promised Blackwood that part of the completed text would follow 'next week', and proposed a further book of collected articles. Quite how Childs survived financially is unclear. In mid-January 1916, he requested an advance on the book because, as he claimed, this would enable him to save about two weeks in its completion. On 12 April, the book still unfinished, Childs addressed the Central Asian Society, where he later became a member. According to him, the invitation to speak had arisen by virtue of his successful connection with '*Maga*' and he clearly regarded the occasion as a significant honour.

Childs's lecture focused on the importance of the Alexandretta Basin in Germany's scheme for dominance in Turkey-in-Asia. The Baghdad Railway was clearly designed to facilitate Germany's war effort but, as Childs recalled, Alexandretta's true significance was as the entrepôt for the exploitation of the economic and strategic potentialities of both Asia Minor and the Arab Middle East; the only port capable of this. As Childs spoke, just a year after concerted British intelligence-gathering activities for a possible landing in Ayas Bay, he drew the attention of his audience to the proximity of parts of the Baghdad Railway to the sea. In his view, Alexandretta was 'the one central spot . . . destined for future greatness' in developing the region. Its possession would confer upon the occupying power the added ability to control railway developments 'between Europe and India and Africa, and largely to Persia'.

Towards the end of July 1916, Childs had decamped to further temporary accommodation, Reigate Villa in Leatherhead, Surrey, his previous lodgings having been closed owing to sudden illness. His failure to complete the book in reasonable time had led him to propose a change of terms so that his publisher would not 'lose out'. However, at the end of August Childs defaulted again on delivery of the book, requesting a further advance as he had no money and no expectation of having earned any by the end of that month. As he observed, 'with the proofs off [his] hands [he] could find something to do but till then he was [fettered]'. By December, two further requests had followed. Yet, Childs was at least actively publicising his book, delivering two well-attended lectures at local venues on Asia Minor and on the Baghdad Railway. He had also suggested two further articles to Blackwood, one on the broad theme of Balkan history and the other on 'Warshrines, Memorials and Muster Rolls', another of his interests.

As Childs informed Blackwood in January 1917, the completion of the book had freed him to look for war work. This search for 'some modest appointment in which I can do service according to my powers', followed a visit to Cherkley Court, the nearby home of the recently ennobled Sir Max Aitken, Lord Beaverbrook. According to Childs, the local medical practitioner, the aptly named Dr Pain, a dinner guest at Beaverbrook's house, where there was a 'week-end party of MPs and Foreign Office people', mentioned Childs when discussion touched on Asia Minor and a car was sent to fetch him. As Childs recalled, the driver wandered up and down 'this pitch-dark country road . . . calling loudly "where is the second house above Springfield Lodge?"'. In a short time, Childs found himself addressing the assembled party in the library of Cherkley Court and talking 'upon Asia Minor and the Baghdad Railway and Greeks and Turks till past midnight'.

In spite of his experience, the British government did not immediately use Childs. Possibly this was owing to intermittent illness, as is indicated by his postponement of a further lecture on the Baghdad Railway. When, late in the year, Childs informed Blackwood that he was to be employed 'in one of the War Intelligence Departments', he had again moved home twice, on the second occasion to 7 Church Street, Leatherhead, where he stayed until at least July 1922. In this time he had again requested an advance, and suggested a further article on historic routes of invasion in Turkey-in-Asia, an offer which he had subsequently to withdraw because of his intelligence duties. Quite what these consisted of in the early days is difficult to establish. He was obliged to improve his knowledge of German in order to secure further work at the Intelligence Department and he was able to do this at home. Yet, by 21 October, Childs had been in camps, training to become an instructor in bombing and trench warfare. Further articles relating to the political aspects of Asia Minor and further lectures were planned, but his anticipated return to a four-day week at the Intelligence Department for the remainder of the winter apparently put paid to these projects; and the articles, on which he had, allegedly, already started work, and which were to have had a more political content, never appeared in the *Proceedings of the Royal Geographical Society*, the intended outlet. Nor, indeed, did the piece on war shrines ever appear in '*Maga*'. The life of the leisured, if impoverished, writer and intelligence gatherer had ended and the remainder of Childs's life and the bulk of his energies as an author and political intelligence analyst were devoted to official duties, first at the Naval Intelligence Department (NID) of the Admiralty and, from July 1919, in precarious employment at the Foreign Office. However, Childs's persistence eventually paid off. The completed book was much to his liking and reviews were uniformly favourable, one of them describing it as 'exceptionally attractive and brilliant'. Childs's only complaint was that Blackwood had not pressed sales in the United States with sufficient vigour.

It seems likely that Childs had been improving his German specifically in order to join Admiralty Intelligence. Prior to and during the first years of the war this organisation had developed much more rapidly than its counterpart housed at the War Office; partly, it seems, as a result of the determination and ability of its chief, Rear Admiral Sir Reginald Hall. By the autumn of 1917, if not earlier, NID had begun preparing very detailed intelligence handbooks for the benefit of policy planning and, as time passed, for the peace preparations when, eventually, these began. When the Historical Section moved to the Foreign Office early in 1918, NID continued to prepare a separate series of geographical handbooks, some of the information in these volumes being used in the main series of Foreign Office *Peace Handbooks*.

From March 1918, Childs appeared in the Confidential *Navy List* in a long list of volunteers or seconded workers in NID. Specifically, he was employed in 'Section 32', the geographical section of NID pioneered by Professor H.N. Dickson of University College, Reading, which was based at Hertford House, Manchester Square, London. His main function was the preparation of handbooks relating to Asia Minor and others relating to the Middle East. One of the former, in particular, in which there were many detailed route plans and a vast amount of information bearing on the geography, history, ethnology and economic aspects of the region, was clearly Childs's work; a photograph of the Cilician Gates being an exact replica of one in *Across Asia Minor on Foot*.

Just how much of a commitment this work represented is difficult to establish, although Childs certainly received very little financial reward. In fact, he received precisely four guineas a week and a railway pass from Leatherhead. Some NID staff were also called upon to contribute to the Foreign Office handbooks being prepared under the supervision of the Historical Section at the Foreign Office. These generally were not attributed and none of the NID handbooks bore signatures. It is clear that highly regarded scholars produced many of the Foreign Office handbooks. A.J. Toynbee, the prolific Balliol scholar, wrote the volume on the Near East. His counterparts at NID, besides Childs, were Professor Calder of the University of Manchester, a classical scholar, who headed the section working on the Near East, James B. Hutton, and Lieutenant E.S. Williams, RN.

At the end of June 1919, Childs co-wrote with Maurice Fanshawe, a specialist in Polish affairs in Section 32, a memorandum entitled 'Population of the Armenian Provinces of the Trans-Caucasia with Maps'. Precisely what first-hand experience Childs had of that region remains unclear. In a memorandum written with J.W. Headlam-Morley in 1924, he recalled having spent part of 1913 in Armenia, but the definition of that region prior to and during the First World War was open to wide interpretation. It is possible that, during the year in which he had allegedly stayed in Samsun, he made forays to the east and into the provinces of so-called Russian Armenia. During his walk from the Black Sea to the Mediterranean, Childs spent some time on the plains of Aleppo and in the Alexandretta Basin, both of which areas were identified by British officials as being a potential homeland for the Armenian people.

Within a month of completing this memorandum with Fanshawe, Section 32 was due to be wound-up. There had already been much speculation regarding its fate. Headlam-Morley, subsequently Historical Adviser to the Foreign Office and Childs's direct superior, considered the question to be one of accommodation, suggesting that the Political Intelligence Department (PID), of the Foreign Office, of which he was Deputy-Director, might offer the best solution. Publicly, Headlam-Morley anticipated a very brief existence but Lord Hardinge, Special Ambassador to the British Peace Conference Delegation, had doubts even on this and was, in any case, wary of the PID. The addition of the proposed ten new members was, in his view, 'unrealistic', and in this he had the backing of the Treasury.

The transfer of Section 32 was not an easy or pleasant time for its members. Blanche Dugdale, another specialist on Polish affairs, felt resentment at their treatment by the authorities. Writing to her uncle Arthur Balfour, the Foreign Secretary, in May 1919, she observed that the Foreign Office would give her colleagues in Section 32 nothing more than 'pious hopes' that they would be used. The issuing of letters of thanks in the following month by the Director of the Intelligence Division to those individuals who had assisted the department during the war, was clearly seen as inadequate recompense. Professor Calder,

Childs and J.B. Hutton, perhaps anxious to maintain their involvement in momentous events, volunteered their services for the summer of 1919, pending the formation of a reconstructed intelligence department of the Foreign Office.

From October 1919, Childs was busy producing monthly reports on Bulgaria, Turkey, Persia, Palestine, Syria, the Caucasus and Transcaspia. Childs, described in one Admiralty document as an 'academic' working for Naval Intelligence, soon had his pay regularised by the Treasury. Yet conditions were not satisfactory. According to one Foreign Office official, the work of Section 32 'would cease absolutely as soon as the Conference ended'. Furthermore, Room 3 or 'The Huts', as their temporary accommodation was known, was evidently considered as being unacceptable by its new occupants. To Childs, however, there were more vital threats to his fledgling career as a Foreign Office analyst. Treasury retrenchments led to a brief termination of his appointment until, finally, in November 1920, the Eastern Department agreed to use him.

Besides preparing monthly reports on developments in the Middle East, Childs also produced occasional memoranda either to answer a specialised point of information or at the specific request of a Foreign Office official or minister. In February 1920, whilst still technically working for Admiralty Intelligence, he wrote a short paper for Robert Vansittart entitled 'Memorandum Respecting the Distribution and Analysis of the Population in the Portion of Bulgaria Ceded to the Allies and in Turkish Thrace, S.E. Europe'.

Further evidence of Childs's interest in and knowledge of Bulgarian and Balkan matters in general, emerged through his involvement in the production of the *History of the Paris Peace Conference*, published jointly in six volumes by the British Institute of International Affairs and Hodder & Stoughton. Childs's contributions, which amounted to roughly sixty-five pages, focused on Bulgaria and the Middle East. For this work he received payment of £27 and his involvement in the project must surely have been a source of pride. Other contributors included Reginald Leeper of the Foreign Office and C.K. Webster, previously employed by a subsection of MI6. The general editor was Harold Temperley, a Cambridge don who spent much of the war as a major in the Intelligence Department of the War Office, MI2. In any case, the project encountered various difficulties and did not fulfil the prediction of publishers Hodder & Stoughton that 'The book is one . . . which statesmen and historians will have to have in their hands centuries hence.'

There is evidence of Childs becoming more involved in the tradition of scholarly civil servants at this time. His membership from 1920 of the Central Asian Society and of the Institute of International Affairs, ensured regular contact with individuals who had travelled in or written on the Near and Middle East. Yet he was not taken into the fold of the Political Intelligence Department or 'Ministry of all the talents', and indeed his identity, position and aspirations as a Foreign Office employee are not entirely clear. Postwar retrenchment and the allure of academia gradually depleted the ranks of the PID and enforced the anxiety of the Foreign Office to reduce staffing levels. Temporary staff such as Childs, who apparently had no outstanding academic achievements to their credit, and who were rather older than those who had such attainments, were particularly vulnerable. Exactly what his status was from the end of 1920 until 1922, when he appeared in the *Foreign Office List* as a temporary clerk in the Eastern Department, is also unclear. His motives for remaining there are likely to have been pecuniary and possibly also related to the attraction of a post where he could apply his experience of travel and intelligence gathering to writing and research. Continuing debate within the Foreign Office about the future of the Political Intelligence and News Departments resulted in the decision to curtail both. Sir William Tyrrell, head of the PID, agreed that the Eastern Department might have Childs. Rex Leeper and Harold Temperley among others were both to follow. In fact, Childs's good fortune in surviving these cutbacks was not shared by some of his colleagues.

Soon after joining the Foreign Office, Childs had apparently begun to plan a further book that would encompass British policy in the Arab Middle East from the first years of the twentieth century. From a later file we know that the first part of the book was to have focused on the Ottoman Empire, part two on Arabia and the Arab regions and part three on Greece. During the period in which this work was in progress, Childs was required to contribute to or compile other papers. Important among these was a long memorandum on Cyprus of December 1924 co-written with Headlam-Morley, by then his direct superior in the Historical Section of the Foreign Office. In it, Childs argued strongly that Britain must not on any count cede the island to Greece. This reflected Childs's opposition, expressed during the war, to the idea of meeting Greek claims in this regard. It was also, as Childs made clear in the memorandum, based upon his own wide-ranging fieldwork in and around the Alexandretta basin in 1912 and 1913 when he had opportunity to study the question on the ground.

More suggestive, perhaps, in terms of Childs's personal experience of Asia Minor, was a memorandum, some thirty pages in length, entitled 'Influence of Pan-Turkish Political Aims on Turkish Military Policy, 1914–1918', written in 1926. Childs's skill as a historian-cum-analyst is well illustrated here. Whilst he confessed that at least some of his analysis was based upon surmise, Childs observed of pre-war German influence in Turkey:

Not often has an ambassador been able to secure, by exercise of his own personality, results so important for his country as Marshall von Bieberstein did for Germany at Constantinople in the early years of this century. . . . I have seen Turkish officers become servile under his glance, though probably they had never seen him before. He gave me the impression of being able to do almost what he liked with Turks.

That Childs, rather than any other eastern specialist attached to government, was asked to write the paper was also suggestive of a 'political' function in Constantinople or, at least, of a developed interest in Turkish political events. Briefly, the paper traced the origins of the pan-Turkish movement and of pan-Islamism and studied the relationship between the former and the Young Turk Movement. It proceeded to analyse the nature of the Turco-German alliance and the military priorities of each power, demonstrating the fundamental divergence of motives both between those countries and within the Turkish leadership in the summer of 1917. Simply stated, Childs argued that Enver aspired primarily to the unification of the Turkish peoples of the Caucasus and Central Asia. Childs claimed that the stirrings of organised Turkish nationalism were evident in Constantinople in 1913 and that his informant at the time, 'a Young Turk', assured him that the 'pan-Turks had formulated a definite policy for the re-creation of their country'.

By 1926, pressure from the Treasury to dispense with Childs's services had intensified. A year later, in July 1927, the Foreign Office was required to provide more detailed evidence of Childs's activities. According to one colleague, Childs 'wr[ote] historical memoranda and deal[t] with special enquiries arising out of political questions concerning the Near East'. Childs received a fixed salary of £750 a year, but Sir Charles Montgomery, an Assistant Under-Secretary at the Foreign Office, doubted that he would be needed for more than another five years, by which time it was expected that the editing of pre-war documents would be completed. Headlam-Morley, who was in overall charge of the project, was due to retire then and it was deemed unlikely that the Foreign Office Library could expand sufficiently to encompass Childs's work as well as his. Late in 1928 further explanations were necessary and Childs was required to describe in detail what progress had been made on the major work upon which he was allegedly employed.

Opinion at the Foreign Office was divided regarding Childs's future. Sir Stephen Gaselee, the distinguished Foreign Office Librarian, considered him to be 'of very great value to the office', but noted that Lancelot Oliphant, head of the Eastern Department, had stated that from the perspective of his department, Childs's continued employment was not essential. Such, also, was the view held by Oliphant when the issue had been discussed in 1925. Headlam-Morley, asked by Gaselee to explain the nature of Childs's regular work, argued that to let Childs go would be 'very bad economy'. As Headlam-Morley added, Childs dealt with a very broad geographical area, encompassing Greece, the Balkans, Asia Minor, the Caucasus, Persia and most areas of the Arab Middle East. He continued:

> The general method adopted is that he should work systematically through some problem, and having done so, should write a formal and connected narrative which will be on record in the Office. He has already written a good deal of this kind – (he is at this moment on leave and I am not able to give you a full account, but will do so later). In regard to many subjects he has done the preliminary work of reading through the records, making notes and compiling a draft – (he has for instance gone carefully through all the records of the Arab Bureau) – but the final stage has not yet been reached.

Difficulties were caused by frequent requests for Childs to undertake other work; ample demonstration, in Headlam-Morley's view, of the value of Childs's 'very special knowledge'. There were many occasions when this knowledge had been indispensable and Headlam-Morley felt it 'quite essential . . . that the Foreign Office should have on its staff someone who ha[d] made himself a master of these extremely complicated affairs'. As Headlam-Morley concluded, the Foreign Office had already recognised the need for such material and the necessity of making 'special provision' for it to be undertaken. In his view, it was vital 'for the proper consideration of current political problems that there should be someone available who has the requisite knowledge'. As Childs alone possessed this

149

knowledge, and was demonstrably capable of expressing himself on paper, Headlam-Morley argued that his services should be retained. If not then the work would have to be done by someone else who lacked Childs's personal experience of the region. Worse still, the work he had produced so far would simply have been wasted.

In his defence, Childs, writing in April 1929, produced a summary paper detailing the nature and completeness of his major historical work, the proposed book on the Near and Middle East in the period 1914 to 1923. His paper was entitled a 'Confidential History of the War in the Near and Middle East; 1914 to 1923'. Childs was under no illusions about the scope of the project. In order adequately to explain the forces at work in the main period of the book, he suggested that it was necessary first to understand the nature of international relations with the Ottoman Empire prior to the First World War. Moreover, in Childs's opinion, it was necessary to perceive that, in making war on Turkey, Britain necessarily faced the issue of tackling possibly hostile Muslim reactions to this throughout her empire and beyond. Childs believed that this 'subject must occupy a great part of th[e] history'.

The overall scheme of the book described by Childs had not changed fundamentally in the decade since its commencement. There were essentially three parts, each one dealing with a separate region. The first covered the Ottoman Empire and the postwar Turkish state. Childs predicted that this section might eventually be comprised of two or even three volumes and that it would deal in a general way with the Anglo-Russian Convention of 1907, with the Turkish Revolution of 1908, with the CUP, with international relations with Turkey, with the Baghdad Railway and the Persian Gulf; and, among other things, with the development of pan-Turanianism, pan-Islamism and pan-Turkism. The nature of Turkish irredentist policies in Persia, Trans- and Cis-Caucasia and the course of events in the Caucasus, including the British occupation, would be the subject of the second volume of the first part. It would also encompass the effect upon Turkey of the Peace Conferences to 1923.

As regards work completed on the first volume, Childs admitted that he had not progressed very far, insofar as the writing of it was concerned. However, he had compiled in note form much of the necessary material and, as he recorded, the necessity of preparing papers regarding specific topics or issues had enabled him to cover a good deal of the ground with regard to the second volume of part one. His problem lay partly in as-yet untapped sources, the archives of the Bolshevik government being a good example. As Childs recorded, he had been learning to read Russian in order to incorporate them.

Greater progress had been achieved with regard to part two of the work which focused on 'Arabia and the Arabian countries'. As Childs noted, the several memoranda submitted by him at various times had enabled him to provide a broad coverage of international relations in the Persian Gulf prior to the First World War and many other kindred subjects detailing British, Turkish and German involvement in the Arab regions of the Middle East.

Part three of the work was to be divided into two sections: the first dealing with Anglo-Greek relations to the fall of Greek premier Venizelos in November 1920 and the second with ensuing events. Little progress had been made on the former but, as he reported, no fewer than 19 chapters plus appendices had been written on the second. As Childs explained, the second volume had advanced more rapidly to take account of Lloyd George's anticipated need for detailed information for the negotiations of 1921.

As he pointed out, he was only then, for the first time since joining the Foreign Office, able to work through the various parts of the proposed work in consecutive order and able to devote his undivided attention to the completion of each section in turn. An estimated completion time of two and a half years seemed realistic to Childs but, as his concluding remarks revealed, he still wished to write for a more general audience. Childs requested that as well as writing the official history he might also produce a further book dealing with 'the last years of the Ottoman Empire, and the rise of the Turkish Republic'. As he continued:

> This work would not be an expurgated text of the official history. Its subject would be the last years of the Ottoman Empire, and the rise of the Turkish Republic. It would deal with the main currents and lights and shades of history, with the origin and sweeping movement of events, with the varying fortunes of the states and peoples involved, and with the personality of the chief rulers and leaders who played their parts in the drama – rather than with high British and allied policy and diplomatic exchanges and secrets.

As Childs acknowledged, he had unrestricted access to documents of the time and permission from the Foreign Office and from the India Office would be required before proceeding.

The result of this debate was a further reprieve but henceforward, Childs was not to be overburdened by requests for memoranda. In future these were to be directed to Gaselee at the Foreign Office Library to which Childs was now to be attached. Typical of the additional demands made on Childs's time was his assistance in the writing and checking of various sections of the Official History of the war. In particular, it seems that Childs had contributed to the history of the Dardanelles Campaign, liaising with the Cabinet Office Historical Section. Similarly, in 1928 to 1929 Childs read and commented upon the chapters on the Near East in Churchill's *History of the Great War*. According to Headlam-Morley, Childs had contributed 'a great deal of valuable information and criticism, which Mr Churchill ha[d] incorporated to a large extent in a revise'. Shortly afterwards, Churchill was moved to enquire as to 'Captain Childs's' opinion of a telegram on the political situation in Turkey. Also, the possibility remains that if, indeed, Childs was ex-SIS, his special knowledge rendered his involvement essential in the preparations and deliberations of the highly secret Interdepartmental

Committee on Eastern Unrest. When, in September 1924, its members discussed the situation in the light of a recent intelligence-gathering mission in Turkey, Childs attended. Also there was Major Vivian, who had charge of SIS operations from Constantinople, and the committee discussed the report of a Captain Pym of MI2 who, with another officer, had been accompanied on their mission by the British military attaché. There were others whose more recent experience perhaps rendered them more indispensable to that body but Childs's ability as an analyst, as one who had accurately plotted the main lines of irredentist Turkish policy, must surely have been an important factor in ensuring his survival at the Foreign Office. The fact that he was not offered permanent employment and that his work was subject to regular scrutiny by the Treasury, was symptomatic of postwar retrenchment.

Childs died from a gastric haemorrhage in 1933. Enquiries were directed to his wife as to the nature of surviving papers left by her husband. According to a minute by M.N. Hughes of the Foreign Office from April 1935, the progress made with his book had been rather disappointing. Yet Childs's contribution to the work of the Foreign Office was not altogether forgotten. His memorandum on the 'Exclusion of Palestine from the Area Assigned for Arab Independence by the McMahon–Hussein Correspondence of 1915–16', was subsequently referred to in glowing terms by Foreign Office officials and others when discussions arose on the Royal Commission on Palestine of 1936. The late Professor Elie Kedourie, the distinguished historian of the Middle East, considered it the most able paper on the subject produced by any British official.

Author's Note

Conclusive evidence of Childs's involvement in intelligence-gathering activities in Ottoman Turkey prior to the First World War has eluded this author. Numerous questions spring to mind.

Why has it proved impossible to find documentary proof of his existence prior to 1915? If Childs was in SIS then why, as an educated and intelligent man, did he find himself in such financial straits soon after his return to England? If Childs was trained to be a trench warfare instructor why has it been impossible to trace him by recourse to military records? Why, indeed, if he was an officer in the services has it proved impossible to trace a military career of any kind? It was certainly unexpected that an idle moment and an irresistible consultation of the Chartwell database – a most unlikely context in which to encounter Childs – was most revealing of all.* Writing of his experiences in Turkey in his critique of some chapters of Churchill's *History of the Great War*, Childs recalled that he had lived in that country from 1909 until almost 1914. The nature of his analysis, together with his memorandum on the pan-Turkish movement, must rate as the strongest evidence for some 'political' function; a position which at least afforded proximity to Turkish officers and politicians and, more especially, to the German Ambassador. Comparison of the routes described in Childs's travel book with the chronology of his stay and with dated track and cart routes detailed in the Admiralty Intelligence Department handbook relating to the Alexandretta region and its approaches, suggests to this author that Childs most probably did have an information-gathering function. There was, indeed, a remarkable coincidence, if in fact it was such, between the timing of Childs's residence in Turkey and the key developments in the negotiations on the Baghdad Railway. All manner of individuals were drawn into the background investigations on this matter and Childs's professed interest in bridges and his lecture on the Baghdad Railway in 1916 strongly support the idea of his involvement in these.

The Secret Intelligence Service, in response to an enquiry from the author as to whether or not Childs was employed by that

---

* The database, at Churchill Archives Centre, indexes parts of the Chartwell Collection, the papers of Sir Winston Churchill.

organisation *prior to or during* the First World War, stated that there was no such record regarding the period from 1914. A note, dated 8 October 1920, relating to a meeting held at the Foreign Office, and at which an unnamed SIS officer attended, is apparently the only available reference to Childs in those parts of the SIS archive consulted by my correspondent. According to that note, Childs was apparently 'responsible for Constantinople'. As regards the period 1909 to 1914, my correspondent was less forthcoming; my query regarding the identity of agent 'C' (initial H), in the payroll for the foreign intelligence-gathering service from April 1909 was met with the rather unsatisfactory suggestion that probably this was the great Sir Mansfield Cumming himself. Regrettably, the true nature of Childs's life may never be revealed, his secret lying hidden somewhere between the Black Sea and the Mediterranean; somewhere, perhaps, on the long road that leads to Baghdad.

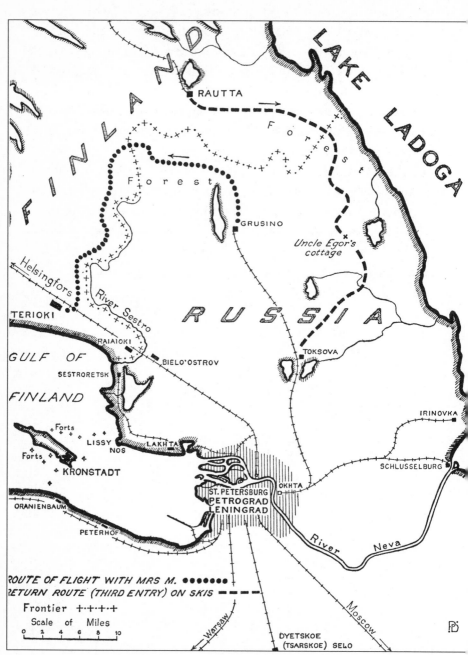

Labels within the map:

LAKE LADOGA

FINLAND

RAUTTA

Forest

Forest

GRUSINO

Uncle Egor's
cottage

Helsingfors

River Sestro

R U S S I A

TERIOKI

RAIAIOKI

TOKSOVA

GULF OF

BIELO'OSTROV

SESTRORETSK

FINLAND

IRINOVKA

Forts

LISSY
NOS

LAKHTA

Forts

SCHLUSSELBURG

KRONSTADT

OKHTA

ORANIENBAUM

ST. PETERSBURG
PETROGRAD
LENINGRAD

PETERHOF

River   Neva

ROUTE OF FLIGHT WITH MRS M. ●●●●●●
RETURN ROUTE (THIRD ENTRY) ON SKIS ━ ━ ━
Frontier +·+·+·+
Scale of Miles
0 2 4 6 8 10

Warsaw

Moscow

DYETSKOE
(TSARSKOE) SELO

5 In and Out of Bolshevik Russia: routes followed by Dukes, from *The Story of 'ST 25*
(*Cassell, 1938*)

6

The Reporter who Played the Piano

COVERT OPERATIONS IN BOLSHEVIK RUSSIA

Glistening snow. Blue-green arc lights swaying in a cutting wind. Grey sentinels huddled in high collars. Silver flashing bayonets jutting from rifles. Train rumbling toward the looming bulk of a frontier station called Kalisch. Gloomy barrenness of a vast, ill-lit waiting-room. Nondescript occupants conversing in whispers. Arctic cold without, stifling heat within. Clouds of steam with each opening of the door.

Voyagers were few on this branch line into Russia of the olden days. Two or three German commercial travellers who had crossed the border with me; a dozen or so local inhabitants awaiting an early train to Lodz or Warsaw; a group of peasants shuffling about awkwardly, apologetically.

Armed guards at each door. . . .

A big, yellow-glassed clock on the dirty buff wall ticked its way to the point of midnight and struck the hour. Outside, distantly, church chimes burst into a fantastic jangle. A waiter in besmeared, ill-fitting tailclothes removed a used-up calendar from the wall and hung up a new one. . . .

The noises in the waiting-room stood out with penetrating intensity. The clock-tick ruled. Spoons in tea-glasses tinkled a surreptitious accompaniment. The waiters took orders mono-syllabically. And sometimes an engine whistle outside shrieked wildly.

With youthful wonderment I imbibed my lemony beverage and the peculiar impressions. Why was I here? Whither bound? Whence hailed? Of the last I thought no more. I was very young, very romantic. The past held little, the future all. Mystery and

157

music were the magnets. The dark and enigmatic Russia of the Tsars – the fairy-tale Russia of Bilibine – the lyric Russia of Rimsky-Korsakov – the passionate Russia of Tschaikovsky – the barbaric Russia of Dostoievsky – these were the Russias that drew me.

Thus begins one of the most gripping narratives of early British espionage. Its author, Paul (later Sir Paul) Dukes, had, two years prior to the events described above, run away from home with only a Gladstone bag. His purpose was to join the Conservatoire in St Petersburg – or Petrograd, as that city was known from 1914. For Dukes, perhaps unusually for a spy, was also an accomplished junior musician. His lack of money meant that, to get to the Russian capital, he had to work his way, often sleeping rough in waiting-rooms like a beggar. There he found a society polarised by wealth or poverty. He personally found native Russians, with whom he lived for some time, 'naïve, illiterate, often barbaric', but in many other ways superior to the nobility who persecuted them. The nature of these early contacts with Russia would alone suggest that he was unusually confident, adventurous, talented and determined for such a young man, qualities that were to stand him in very good stead in the following years. In St Petersburg he felt at home immediately. On his arrival there he went straight to the Conservatoire and was admitted as a student. There he came under the influence of Albert Coates – 'a remarkable and lovable man and a great musician' – who had recently been made conductor at the Imperial Marinsky Opera.

Quite soon after the outbreak of war, British officials identified Dukes's exceptional talents. He was by then fluent in the Russian language, had formed useful contacts in Petrograd, and had already formed a bond with the country and its people. In October 1915 he was asked to join the newly formed Anglo-Russian Commission under Hugh (later Sir Hugh) Walpole and Harold Williams, who was an accomplished Russian linguist. The nature of the duties attached to this position, which involved following the Russian press all over the country, a 'prodigious task', led to his resignation from the Marinsky Theatre early in 1916. As Dukes recorded, the growth of the Zemstvo unions and the co-operative movement in the war had produced a huge increase in the number of newspapers.

Certainly there was no doubting Dukes's abilities as a reporter. Recalling, in his book, a meeting with Rasputin when he shared a flat with Sidney Gibbes, the English tutor of the Tsarevitch, his abilities as a narrative writer emerge:

> He was dressed in a blue silk Russian shirt . . . a Russian coat of country pattern, black breeches and top boots. Long hair protruded from beneath his cap. A shaggy beard hid his neck in front. But his rat-like eyes, darting in every direction, were rightly described as his most striking feature. It was unbelievable that this coarse peasant was the uncrowned Tsar of all the Russias, and that courtiers and ladies bearing the highest titles in the land cringed before him, accompanied him at his beck and call, even to the baths, and to show their devotion would lick his fingers at the dinner-table, even in the presence of others, when he had finished eating with his hands because he did not know how to use a knife and fork. . . . Rasputin merely resembled a boil – a symptom of the poisons lurking in the blood of the Russian political and social organism. Rasputin was possible because Russian society was rotten. Had the fester broken out in some other form the revolution would have been just as inevitable. . . . Bitter resentment grew into hatred, and loud were the protests against the 'dark forces' that held Russia in their grip.

No less remarkable was the fact that, having mastered the Russian language in the eight years or so since he had arrived in Russia, Dukes was already able to observe events at the very centre, having successfully gained the confidence both of potential allies and foes alike. He was also passionate about the emerging political developments in the vast, sprawling empire, in the throes of war, hunger and riots, where he detected a 'fast-growing spirit of revolt, approaching boiling-point'. When the moment came, first on 11 March 1917, Dukes was there to witness the first spill of blood on the glittering snow:

> The Nevsky Prospect – the Champs Elysées of Petrograd, as St. Petersburg had been renamed in 1914 – was almost deserted. The air was tense with excitement, and it seemed as if from the girdling *faubourgs* rose a low, muffled rumbling as of many voices. Angry, passionate voices, rolling like distant thunder, while in the heart of the city all was still and quiet. A mounted patrol stood here or there, or paced the street with measured step. There were bloodstains on the white snow, and from the upper end of the Prospect still resounded the intermittent crack of rifles.

As Dukes recalled, next day his fears were borne out. The first revolutionary regiments were despatched and he saw the crowds sack the government arsenal. Soldiers burst into Kresty Prison. From above, machine-gun fire sprayed the watching crowd. Further crowds surged around the Duma. From there, late that night, Dukes managed to climb the gates, run through the bushes and reach the building.

Over the following days, Dukes observed political developments intently. The Provisional government, the Soviet, Kerensky, the people and the Bolsheviks all seemed to pull in different directions. As Lenin stepped off the train that had brought him from Switzerland, he was observed by Dukes, who claimed to have seen a 'certain look' in the eyes of his supporters, that made him, Dukes, 'hurry home'.

Besides his official duties, Dukes had also been covering for his journalist friend Arthur Ransome as special correspondent of the *Daily Chronicle*. Although, as Dukes claimed, his friends in Russia derided him for his belief that Lenin and his henchmen would one day occupy positions of power, 'their names . . . began to reverberate across revolutionary skies like rising peals of thunder'. Suddenly, in the summer of 1917, this period of intense excitement appeared to be at an end, for Dukes was asked to become special liaison officer between the Anglo-Russian Commission and the Foreign Office.

From Room 7 of the Foreign Office in London, Dukes analysed and commented on mounds of papers and despatches, working late into the night. When a Zeppelin raid was signalled, he ignored warnings to retreat to the basement and instead stood in the darkness 'at a window overlooking St James's Park, fascinated by the swaying beams of searchlights, by the *crescendo–sforzando–smorzando* of the roaring invaders high up in the black heavens, by the crack of guns and the boom of bombs. And in the morning I returned to my desk laden with papers.' Dukes's appointment introduced him to men of importance such as Lord Carson and John Buchan, who headed the Department of Information. It also took him to France, to examine intercepted correspondence of the Bolshevik leaders, and to the Western Front to examine 'various auxiliary organizations serving the soldiers' and analyse their potential use on the Russian Front. On his return to the Foreign Office in November 1917, he found a 'sheaf of sensational despatches' that he read avidly. Although highly regarded by his superiors as a liaison officer, Dukes was determined to return to Russia where, it seemed, the revolutionary spirit had turned ugly, and the moderate politicians now languished in jail:

The horror of the Flanders front was echoed in the streets at home, and now was added the horror in the streets of Petrograd and Moscow – dealt by hands sent back to Russia by those who were dropping these bombs upon the women and children of London. If only I, too, could have been a fighter! If only I, too, could have gone 'over the top'! But my sorry lot was to be in mufti. As a needed 'specialist', I had even been torn away from my base of operations – and was expected to comment upon reports that were now days old – months old, if calculated in revolutionary time.

His superiors, or at least one of them, John Buchan – the author, as Dukes recalled, of *Greenmantle* – was sympathetic and permitted Dukes to make his own arrangements to return to Russia. In December 1917, with the passport of a King's Messenger, and diplomatic bags for delivery to embassies in Oslo, Stockholm and Petrograd, Dukes 'was sent off on a roving commission . . . to inquire into the possibilities of relief work in the new Russia where distress was already rife, and at the same time to report on whatever I saw wherever I went'. As Dukes also recalled, this mission was also the precursor of his formal entry into the Secret Intelligence Service or MI1c as it was then known.

For the first half of 1918, Dukes roamed over Russia observing relief measures, but he felt increasingly drawn to the more urgent and compelling political developments and to the widespread confusion that met his eyes. As he recalled, the Bolsheviks planned to sign a peace with Germany and were rapidly disposing of their enemies. Decrees – prohibiting buying and selling, declaring private property to belong to the Communist Party – were issued daily. Food and fuel were in critical shortage and transport was seizing up. In town and country alike, the tentacles of Bolshevik rule were gradually extended, whether in the form of the fast proliferating committees or the *Cheka*, the secret police, 'which searched, seized, and shot, at will'.

Then, in June 1918, the British Consul-General in Moscow cabled Dukes that the Foreign Office wanted him to return to London immediately. This he accomplished by White Sea steamer via Archangel, Murmansk, Petchenga, by tug to the Norwegian frontier, through the fjords to Bergen by the North Cape, across the North Sea and finally to Scotland. There, in Aberdeen, the resident MI5 officer passed him on to the first train to London. At King's Cross – slightly bemused by the speed of his recall – he was whisked by car to a 'side street in the vicinity of Trafalgar

Square'. After an obstacle course of 'rabbit burrow-like passages, corridors, nooks and alcoves, piled higgledy-piggledy on the roof', a roof-top iron bridge, and a further maze of passages, his chauffeur, 'with mask-like face', led him to a tiny room 'where sat an officer in the uniform of a British colonel'. There, much to his surprise, Dukes was asked if he would work for the Secret Intelligence Service and was given until the following day to consider his decision.

On the next day, exhilarated, Dukes was introduced to the head of the political section of MI1c, a friend of the master spy Sidney Reilly, who had some years earlier been involved in tracking down an anarchist plot hatched in Switzerland and financed in Germany for the assassination of all of the heads of Allied countries.

Without delay, Dukes was told of his new rôle. He was to report from Russia on general conditions, changes of policy, the attitude of the population, military and naval matters, possibilities for an alteration of regime, and what Germany was doing. How he was to re-enter the country, under what cover he would live, and how his reports should be exfiltrated, was left to him. As Dukes recalled, with some anticipation, he was also ushered in to see the Chief:

From the threshold the room seemed bathed in semi-obscurity. Against the window everything appeared in silhouette. A row of half a dozen extending telephones stood at the left of a big desk littered with papers. On a side table were maps and drawings, with models of aeroplanes, submarines and mechanical devices, while a row of bottles suggested chemical experiments. These evidences of scientific investigation only served to intensify an already over-powering atmosphere of strangeness and mystery.

But it was not these things that engaged my attention as I stood nervously waiting. It was not the bottles or the machinery that attracted my gaze. My eyes fixed themselves on the figure at the writing-table. . . .

This extraordinary man was short of stature, thick-set, with grey hair half covering a well-rounded head. His mouth was stern, and an eagle eye, full of vivacity, glanced – or glared, as the case might be – piercingly through a gold-rimmed monocle. The coat that hung over the back of his chair was that of a naval officer.

Thus Dukes described Sir Mansfield Cumming, a man whom he found initially severe, but, on closer inspection, a 'British officer and an English gentleman of the very finest stamp, fearless, gifted with limitless resources of subtle ingenuity'. Though willing to provide training in ciphers, Cumming made it clear that, once Dukes had crossed into Russia and particularly if he were caught, his organisation would be unable to do anything to help. After a night-time rendezvous at Kingston Station in Surrey, Dukes left for Newcastle and a vessel which took him to Archangel, which was then occupied by Allied troops.

As Dukes recalled, he was returning to what was certainly a new environment if not a new country. For one thing it was a hostile country with which Britain was at war. Among other things, the Bolsheviks now ruled with violence and terror and had murdered the Russian royal family. Further, an attempt had been made on Lenin's life, the 'Lockhart Plot' had heightened tensions, and anti-Bolshevik forces were gathering in Archangel, Finland, Siberia and south Russia. During an assault on the British Embassy by the *Cheka*, the British naval attaché, Captain Cromie, had been killed. In Archangel, Dukes lived incognito, his existence known only to a few very senior British officers. He lived quietly, attempting to grow a beard that would assist his disguise. He also trained hard, hoping that he might be able to reach the capital by virtue of an arduous trip over moors and lakes. However, the weather broke and Dukes, forced to adopt another approach, instead disguised himself as a Norwegian travelling salesman, journeying from Norway to Stockholm. There, helped by a senior intelligence officer, he became a Serb – Sergei Ilitch, 'travelling for business to Helsingfors'. From there, in early November 1918, Dukes moved to Viborg near the Finnish–Russian border, a 'hornets' nest of refugees, conspirators, German agents and Bolshevist spies'. There he was introduced to a Russian officer, Melnikov, who agreed to arrange his crossing of the border. The meeting was, as Dukes admitted, 'providential'. Melnikov, though a committed monarchist, was nonetheless utterly dependable and, following the murder of his parents by the Bolsheviks, fervently opposed to the new regime. Melnikov also informed Dukes of the existence in Petrograd of a businessman, whose aliases included John Johnovitch or Ivan Ivanitch. Armed with a password for the Finnish border patrol, a heavily disguised Melnikov left for Bolshevik Russia.

Dukes's own crossing of the border was highly dangerous and suspenseful. The Finnish guards, though anxious to help, were deeply aware of the danger of detection. The woodland on the Russian side of the frontier was heavily patrolled and the direction and timing of the patrols varied to catch the unwary. Bedraggled in his long hair and beard and disguised, of all things, as a *Cheka* agent by the name of Joseph Ilitch Afirenko, Dukes found himself about to cross the frontier over a stream in a boat in the middle of the night. He carried extra socks, handkerchiefs, dry biscuits and whisky. It was freezing cold, and although he managed to push the boat to the opposite bank, his landing was clumsy. Stepping onto the bank, he crashed through the ice, a light appeared, shots and shouting followed, and Dukes lay undetected in the deep snow. After a cold and dangerous night in the outdoors, on the following day he caught a train for Petrograd.

Dukes, whatever he thought of his own abilities in this regard, was undoubtedly a natural intelligence agent. Though prepared to admit his complete lack of experience, by the time of his return to Russia he had risked his life repeatedly and had proved himself a master of disguise; something that was to distinguish his period of Secret Service work. In Petrograd and in Moscow, he later noted that he had used at least twenty different disguises. This was essential not only for his own safety but also to protect the network of individuals who sheltered him at one time or another. Though obviously brave and physically tough, he was also completely honest about his fears. As he left Viborg by train, he confessed to feeling under constant scrutiny and 'shivered and was ready to curse myself for my fool adventure'. When about to cross the border itself in the dead of night, he recalled: 'The bushes around seemed silently alive, the stooping men ahead of me were from another world. There are single moments for which, out of aeons of time, we are called upon to live. This was one of them for me. There were to be many more. It was as well that I could not foresee them. It was as well that I went blindly, out of a sense of duty as much as curiosity or love of adventure.' It was precisely that curiosity to discover the views of ordinary people that compelled him to return to Russia – whatever the cost.

Arriving in Petrograd, which he found in a progressive state of decay, Dukes was immediately put to the test. Having gone to visit Ivanitch, Dukes discovered too late that the house was guarded. When challenged, as he was to be on many future occasions, his sharpness of mind alone saved him from more detailed probing. On that occasion he claimed to have brought a parcel of Ivanitch's belongings which the latter – whom he claimed not to know – had left behind at a friend's house. In fact, soon after his return, Dukes felt an oppressive weight of being everywhere in disguise and of being unable to return openly to greet old friends who, admittedly, in many cases had been imprisoned or forced to flee. There was also a perennial need for watchfulness and, despite his identity papers, of not being caught unawares by a *Cheka* raid. This need for shelter took him to the flat of one Sereievitch Alexandrovna, a friend of Melnikov, where he was reunited with the latter and also met Ivanitch or, as he called him thereafter, Murometz. The latter, a giant of a man, had recently narrowly escaped police custody by descending a drainpipe outside his kitchen window. The Bolshevik agents were now close on his trail and he had resolved to escape

rather than imperil his associates further. Later, Murometz and Dukes were able to talk freely. Murometz had lost his country farm and had long been suspected by the *Cheka* of assisting the escape of Allied nationals. Yet he would not leave, the more so now that several of his entourage, including one who was referred to simply as 'Madame M.', had been taken hostage by the police.*
Murometz had a wide network of associates and, apparently, an ever-ready supply of cash. One of these associates, a former policeman whom Murometz used to gain knowledge of her – described by Dukes as 'short, red-faced and insignificant-looking' – was able to report that Madame M. was being subjected to lengthy interrogations.

Then, one day, Dukes learned that Melnikov had been arrested. His informant was a Russian officer by the name of Zorinsky, whom he had met on the day of his arrival. Zorinsky, with whom Dukes occasionally stayed and dined, was a deeply sinister and cunning man who one evening told Dukes that he had an interest in counter-espionage. An interest, which, with a lopsided grin, he suggested, Dukes shared, being in the same line of work. Zorinsky had then handed Dukes a report on highly confidential negotiations between the Bolshevik government and the leaders of non-Bolshevik parties with a view to forming a coalition government. He also promised to provide further information as, he claimed, he had done for Captain Cromie, the British naval attaché who had been murdered during a *Cheka* assault on the British Embassy. As Dukes later discovered, his suspicions of Zorinsky were well founded.

Dukes also faced other dangers, principal among them being the *Cheka* under the merciless Felix Dzerzhinsky, 'an instrument of national espionage such as the world had never before seen'. As Dukes recalled, they 'practised every invention of exquisite

---

* In his earlier book, *Red Dusk and the Morrow*, and in an article in *The Times*, Dukes referred to her as Mrs Lydia Marsh, the wife of Murometz, whom he called 'Marsh'.

villainy to extract from captives the secrets of their accomplices'. Yet knowing this, Dukes used every possible means to obtain information about the workings of its equally forbidding headquarters. Such were conditions there that its inmates, housed in dank, icy cellars, were relieved if, during the 'terror-hour', when the guards fetched the condemned, their names were called for the 'merciful bullet' rather than endure the 'drawn-out torment of the dungeon'. Meanwhile, the policeman, 'excessively vain and boastful', who lived in 'abominable conditions . . . conditions too loathsome for words', did at least provide information about Madame M., whose interrogation by the *Cheka* had now left her at breaking point. The preferred methods of that organisation consisted of repeated interrogations by different inquisitors until the captive collapsed. Then they would feed them with salt herring and deprive them of water, flog them, fire blank cartridges at their heads, or drive needles under their nails. Murometz confessed that his own capture was imminent and he arranged his departure, entrusting the problem of Madame M. to Dukes. Accompanying the heavily disguised businessman to the station, Dukes recorded his despondency:

> I stood and watched it [the train] pass into the darkness, and, as it vanished, the cold, the gloom, the universal dilapidation seemed to become intensified. I listened to the distant rumble until I found myself alone upon the platform. Then I turned, and as I slowly retraced my steps into town an aching sense of emptiness pervaded everything, and the future seemed nothing but impenetrable night.

After an eventful and nerve-racking journey, Murometz himself escaped safely across the Finnish border, and Dukes was later able to communicate a letter to him written in invisible ink.

Life in Petrograd was equally taut. There were frequent hold-ups and searches, Dukes only being spared by virtue of his *Cheka* passport. Although his assumed identity provided him with better rations, these had to be shared among his hosts and informants and there were constant dangers to deal with. Besides meeting with these contacts, Dukes also attended public meetings and read widely in the Soviet literature and press. There was also danger from *Cheka* agents listening into telephone conversations, making it necessary for Dukes and his informants to speak in metaphor or by means of 'prearranged verbal signals'.

Zorinsky had also been causing Dukes some concern. At their frequent meetings, their conversations increasingly took the form of a cat-and-mouse game. Zorinsky, after all, had provided Dukes with genuinely useful intelligence and had been helpful in other respects. On the other hand, his open and friendly manner might equally have been a ploy to draw Dukes out and reveal his own identity and that of his helpers, Murometz especially. In fact, when Dukes told him of Murometz's escape, Zorinsky was initially 'livid' and stated that the hostages, for whom Murometz had shown much concern, would undoubtedly be shot. Uncertain of how to proceed, Dukes played along with Zorinsky's plan of securing the release of Madame M. by bribing the investigator. Though the sum was desperately high, Dukes could not compromise himself with Zorinsky. Having given him half of the money, Dukes had in the meantime coaxed the policeman – notwithstanding his personal shortcomings – to arrange a plan for her release. According to this plan, Dukes was to wait for Madame M. outside the prison at 4 p.m. on 18 December. As he recalled, the day 'dawned bleak and raw. The wind tore in angry gusts round the corners of the houses, snatching up the snow and flinging it viciously in the half-hidden faces of hurrying, harassed pedestrians.' Dukes and an accomplice bought a cloak for Madame M., who appeared at the appointed hour. She had been called as if for an interrogation but was instead directed to the women's lavatory where she found a pass. With this she was able to leave the prison. Without delay and after a brief stop at Murometz's flat, they reached the railway station. Dukes told Madame M. that if challenged they were to claim to be 'speculators'. The train was soon 'packed to suffocation' and after several hours, just before midnight, arrived at Grusino, within striking distance of the border with Finland. There, as instructed by Murometz, Dukes led Madame M. to the house of a collaborator who had aided Murometz's escape. From there, Dukes, Madame M., and several other escapees, set out. It was a beautiful, moonlit night. From a further hut in a forest clearing five miles from the frontier, the party walked slowly with a guide through deep snowdrifts, winding in and out of the cover provided by the forest. Two of the party (young girls of about fifteen and seventeen) were daughters of the Grand Duke Paul Alexandrovitch, uncle of the Tsar. Madame M. was told to say only that Dukes was a Swedish refugee. At one point, encountering an impassable ditch full of ice and water, Dukes had to form a bridge with his body to allow the party to cross. As Dukes noted, it was only three weeks since his perilous journey into Finland, yet so immersed had he become in his new rôle that it was the outside world into which he emerged that now appeared strange.

Before going to the British Legation in Helsingfors, Dukes, ever anxious to blend into the crowd, visited a barber, having his luxuriant beard trimmed to a goatee to allow him to revert quickly to his original disguise. From Helsingfors he travelled to Stockholm and spent Christmas there with the head of British Intelligence in the region, whom Dukes referred to tantalisingly as 'Major S'. That officer may well have been the Major Scales or 'ST 27' who had previously served in Russia in an intelligence capacity. Dukes also learned to his satisfaction that his reports smuggled out by Murometz and subsequent escapers had reached London and were much appreciated by the Foreign Office. Once again, however, Dukes felt the urge to return and complete his task. Dressed in a green overcoat, his pockets stuffed with cigarettes, chocolate and several flasks of whisky, the Finnish border patrol again smuggled Dukes into Russia. At the crucial moment of running across the moonlit clearing at the border, Dukes wrapped himself loosely in a white sheet to minimise the chances of being detected.

On his return to Petrograd, Dukes found that the Bolsheviks were pressing people to military service and it became vital for him to obtain exemption if he were to keep in touch with political developments. In conversation with the sinister Zorinsky, it emerged that the latter somehow knew of Dukes's trip to Finland and of his escape with Madame M. He produced, as if by magic, a naval chart showing the location of all of the mines in the Gulf of Finland, claiming that Dukes might copy it if he wished. Dukes rightly sensed himself being slowly enmeshed. Aware that Dukes, as a spy, must have military exemption certificates, Zorinsky produced one for himself and another, unsigned, which he offered to Dukes. Dukes realised that he must sign the documents in front of Zorinsky. His brain worked desperately to avoid divulging the identity under which he was living. The 'clever, cynical, mysterious Zorinsky' had ensnared him. As he completed the document Dukes was obliged to produce his *Cheka* passport and reveal his alias. As Dukes recalled he could not help but feel that he had compromised his safety by his hesitancy and, more especially, by showing his *Cheka* passport to Zorinsky that evening.

While pacing his room that night, he decided he would at least try to make his exemption certificate appear used. As he folded it repeatedly, cracks appeared and it became clear that, unknown to Zorinsky, there were two copies of the form stuck together. Dukes now only needed a new passport to be quite free of Zorinsky. He obtained it via Melnikov's uncle, a doctor on the islands, who, in turn, maintained contact with friends of Melnikov in the anti-Bolshevik movement. The passport, in the name of Alexander Markovitch, post office clerk, soon had a military exemption certificate to match, and was valid for three months.

Dukes's disguises were evidently convincing. When visiting his old quarters, where he was known to his housekeeper by his real English name, she refused to admit him and it was only when he had returned with a hastily written letter purporting to be from

Dukes and asking him to visit his flat, that she admitted him. Also, as Dukes recalled, when examining the dilapidated state of his flat he saw a picture of himself: '. . . I was struck by the completeness of my present disguise. How different I now appeared in my beard, long hair and glasses.' From his belongings there and various markets he assembled an outfit that suited his position as a postal official. Also, he meticulously built up a network of reliable contacts who might provide occasional sleeping quarters to make his habits less predictable.

Then, from enquiries made with the policeman, Dukes discovered that Melnikov had been executed some weeks previously. This was a great shock as, apart from losing a dependable ally, he had hoped to use Melnikov considerably in his work. It also seemed to confirm his worst fears about Zorinsky. It became imperative to have a 'breathing-space', just as it was vital to escape the clutches of Zorinsky and the *Cheka*. Further, Dukes had lost two reliable couriers and he wished to report to his intelligence chiefs. To this end, close to midnight on a 'dark and windless night', Dukes sat in a hut on the edge of the frozen Gulf of Finland in a suburb of Petrograd, ready to escape once again. On this occasion, his plan was to lie under some hay in a smuggler's sleigh and be driven west over the ice along the Finnish coast. Dukes recalled what happened next:

In a moment we were flying at breakneck speed over the ice, which was windswept after recent storms. The half-inch of frozen snow on the surface just sufficed to give grip to the horse's hoofs. Twice, bumping into snow ridges, we capsized completely. When we got going again the runners sang like a saw-mill. The driver noticed this too, and was alive to the danger of being heard from shore; but his sturdy pony, exhilarated by the frosty air, was hard to restrain.

As the sleigh approached Kronstadt, the beams of searchlights flickered across their path and the driver directed the pony towards the mainland. Too close, however, and in a moment Dukes realised they were being pursued. Neither bribery nor the threat of being shot, to which Dukes resorted to make the driver go faster, had any effect and in a moment, amid gunshots, he lost control and the sleigh was surrounded. With seconds to spare, Dukes slid 'eel-like' onto the snow and towards the shore. In his hand he carried documents that, if he were caught, he would throw away into the darkness or otherwise face immediate death. Unable to reach the shore in time, Dukes hurled himself down onto a black icy patch where, in the darkness, his body made no impression. 'Here they were now – close at hand – thud of hoofs muffled by crisp snow – short shouts lost on the night air. They rode so close that it seemed that one of them *must* ride over me.' But his assailants did not see Dukes and gave up the chase and he, wet and exhausted, haltingly dragged himself to the Finnish shore and found shelter of sorts behind a disused shed. There he was discovered on the following morning by a Finnish patrol, which promptly dragged him off to the Commandant at Terioki for interrogation.

With a great deal of difficulty Dukes managed to persuade his interrogators that he was not a Bolshevik spy and that the Commandant, whose sympathies lay with Germany rather than with Britain, should refer to a higher authority. Having duly rested and conveyed his reports to the Acting Consul at Helsingfors, Dukes was eager to return. His chiefs apparently did not expect this though it is clear just how exclusive was the information he supplied. A memorandum of the Political Intelligence Department of the Foreign Office from this time made it clear that Dukes alone provided the raw intelligence of events in Petrograd and Moscow. His friend Arthur Ransome had remained in Moscow only very briefly and the only other British man to stay in Russia in an independent capacity had also now left after a brief stay. In any case, the latter was a journalist and his information was destined for the English press. At least, as Dukes learned, his reports were being circulated to British

Missions at, among other centres, Stockholm, Helsingfors, Reval, Riga, and Warsaw. Each of them was on standby to provide Dukes assistance and, as 'Major S' told Dukes, MI1c was preparing 'very special measures' to enable Dukes to leave Petrograd at short notice.

Having given the Commandant at the frontier the slip, Dukes befriended a Finnish Army officer en route to assume command of the garrison on a border village. With provisions of chocolate, condensed milk and various other useful commodities, Dukes was led by a guide on a hazardous night-time ski run towards the frontier:

> We stopped frequently to listen for suspicious sounds, but all that greeted our ears was the mystic and beautiful winter silence of a snow-laden northern forest. The temperature was about twenty degrees below zero, with not a breath of wind, and the pines and firs, bearing their luxuriant white burden, looked as if a magic fairy wand had lulled them into perpetual sleep. . . . We moved noiselessly but for the gentle swish of our skis which scarcely broke the stillness, and the stars that danced above the tree-tops smiled down upon us approvingly.

At the frontier they paused, listening and watching intently for movement. With a sudden push, Dukes's guide sped across the open space and disappeared into the trees on the other side. Dukes followed safely. After several miles and, on Dukes's part, an almost disastrous attempt to jump across a water-filled dyke, they arrived safely at the village that was his intended destination. Though otherwise intact, Dukes's feet were badly frostbitten. Entering the village and unable to find his guide, Dukes knocked on the door of one of the first houses. His good fortune continued. The occupants of the house – a peasant family who shared his passion for music – took him under their wing and, having rested briefly, Dukes journeyed with them towards Petrograd.

Back at Melnikov's flat, he learned that soldiers had come for him that morning and had used the name Krylenko, one of his most recent and commonly used aliases. It became vital to change his appearance, and he headed for a safe house, limping as his frostbitten feet began to swell. Entering the building, having first observed it closely, he approached the stairs. Then, suddenly, he heard the lock of the flat being picked on the floor above. He could hear whispered conversation. He fled, but lost his footing and found a revolver against his head. With lightning reactions, Dukes affected stupidity, pretending to have mistaken the number of the house for the one he wanted. Dukes, badly shaken, limped off, watched intently by his assailant. As he recalled, 'it was one of those moments when I hated my job'.

In considerable pain, Dukes eventually found sanctuary with Melnikov's uncle, the doctor, and there had his feet bandaged, his beard removed and his hair cut. To the amazement of the doctor, he unpicked some stitching from the lapel of his coat and extracted a false tooth, which he proceeded to insert in a gap that, in various guises, had previously distinguished his appearance. As he recalled, he presented the 'appearance of a clean-shaven, short-haired, tidy but indigent, ailing and underfed "intellectual"'. Such was the success of the disguise that he went unrecognised by previous associates. One of these was a close friend of Melnikov, and when Dukes had persuaded him as to his identity, he was able to tell Dukes of Zorinsky's murky past as a disgraced Army officer, an embezzler and cheat, who had turned to double-dealing with the *Cheka* and with anti-revolutionary forces. It seems that he had betrayed Melnikov and had also, by means of the telephone operator, discovered where Dukes, as the Krylenko in his false passport, lived. As long as Dukes paid him, or there remained a chance of discovering a wider network of anti-Bolshevik forces, he would not have betrayed him. However, the moment it suited Zorinsky's purposes, Dukes would have been shot.

With his new identity and making every effort to avoid his old haunts, Dukes was temporarily safe. Zorinsky had gone to

Finland to track him down, but would there only find evidence to confirm Dukes's identity as Krylenko rather than any trace of Alexander Markovitch. In fact, Dukes was quickly immersed in a new mode of life in the emerging political situation and had more than enough to occupy his mind.

Within a fortnight of his return and reinvention as Markovitch, Dukes was faced with further opportunities for intelligence gathering. In March 1919, in an effort to quell the sudden eruption of strikes and anti-Bolshevik demonstrations, Lenin addressed a rally in the People's Palace where, unknown to him, he was closely observed by a heavily disguised agent of the British government. At great personal risk, Dukes had obtained a pass and, feigning even greater disability than was the case, he was accompanied by a member of the Communist Party. That individual, quite unaware of Dukes's true identity or purposes, aided him at every stage. In fact, such was Dukes's success in this new guise that when, in ensuing months, the Comintern or Communist International emerged, he was asked to become one of its missionaries abroad. His physical weakness was ascribed by his associates to a period of imprisonment in England where he and his father had been exiled by the Tsarist regime because of their advanced views. Whilst a proselytising mission of this kind might have offered a convenient means of escape, Dukes's mission was not completed.

There can be little doubt that part of Dukes's success as an agent was due to his quick brain and his ability, based on his skill at languages, his disguise and acting techniques, to remain calm and convincing in any situation. Also, as he was later to emphasise when the British Treasury refused payments to some of his helpers, he had the firm support not only of many Russians, who looked to Britain to intervene in Russia and liberate Petrograd, but also of the small but deeply patriotic British community. Both groups were implacably opposed to Bolshevik rule, although not, in Dukes's case at least, to the principles of that system. Beyond this, Dukes also had a gift of friendship.

Whether he was being sincere or not he seemed to fit in. In many cases, he formed very deep personal attachments to his helpers. In the case of one English collaborator, George Edward Gibson, a businessman who repeatedly financed his work, he was in 1921 prepared publicly to embarrass the British Foreign Office and Secret Service, when the Treasury refused to repay money which he had lent Dukes.

The nature of these loyalties was also illustrated by Dukes's account of his dealings with some anti-Bolshevik Russian naval officers. These officers worked clandestinely to organise the transfer to Archangel or to the frontier of officers who wished to join the British and to stir up a mutiny at the Kronstadt naval base as a preparation for the anticipated arrival of the Allied and Finnish forces. Dukes met their leader, 'the Admiral', and maintained contact through an officer called Kolya Orlov. They had no funds as such but made their money by raiding Bolshevik treasuries of possessions that the Bolsheviks had taken from them in the first place. From the story that followed – the betrayal and death of three of their number during such a raid – it was clear that Dukes held them in very high personal regard and had developed powerful loyalties and friendships with them.

Dukes also developed a strong attachment to an elderly lady with whom he lodged, and whom he referred to as Aunt Natalia, whose presence of mind on at least one occasion saved him from detection by *Cheka* patrols. She also provided an ingenious solution to the problem of where Dukes should store his backlog of intelligence reports which awaited a courier, suggesting that Dukes bury them in her family plot in Smolensk cemetery. As Dukes later confessed, Aunt Natalia's near death from starvation, the thought of her suffering and her eventual arrest and execution by the Bolsheviks had on several occasions reduced him to tears. The police patrols were stepped up; even greater vigilance was required, and each night Dukes hid a small rubber bag containing his secret papers in a toilet cistern. In fact, Aunt Natalia's flat became his main refuge for three months, although he was constantly building up new contacts and testing old and reliable ones to see if they could be renewed. On such occasions he would either pretend to be the brother of the man they had known or else simply adopt a new disguise. A second search of Aunt Natalia's flat and the fact that the *Cheka* officer leading the search had made a note of Dukes's details – as his papers were due for renewal – meant that he had to seek alternative lodgings. The search was part of a concerted effort by the *Cheka* to round up anti-Bolshevik elements following the failed advance on Petrograd by White troops in Estonia.

Tension was again mounting in the capital. There were rumours of a rising in Kronstadt and a nightly curfew was imposed after 10 p.m. As his feet healed, Dukes no longer had a good reason for visiting the doctor, and, when the latter's house was raided, he was forced to dispose of his identity papers. Somehow, and Dukes again suspected Zorinsky, the *Cheka* had got wind of his new disguise and had been searching for the 'frostbitten Englishman'. Unable to return to the doctor's flat and refused entry by another contact, Dukes was forced to sleep outside, finding peace if not great comfort in the shell of a tomb in the neglected Volkovo cemetery. He also encountered, quite by chance, the courier whose arrival he had long awaited, Peter Petrovich. The latter explained that, when the time was right, Dukes would be taken out of Petrograd by means of a newly developed, high-powered torpedo launch captained by a British officer. Lieutenant R.N. Agar, it seems, had been summoned to the headquarters of MI1c and was recruited to assist Dukes's escape. The torpedo boat was capable of travelling at very high speeds and it was agreed that if, as London wished, Dukes were able to stay on for a short time, Agar would return on three prearranged dates to collect him. The first, besides a meeting forty-eight hours from that date, would be in approximately five weeks' time. Later, lying in the broken tomb, Dukes considered himself much safer than many in the city itself:

Thousands tonight in the big city would be watching and waiting and listening in terror lest the thundering lorries, feverishly conveying bayoneted Chekisti hither and thither, should stop at *their* house, and *their* door receive the dreaded knock. Thousands would sit up sleepless and trembling, never knowing whether some accidental circumstance, some chance remark even of their own kith and kin, some suggestion wormed out of their own children, might not have cast suspicion upon them. Useless then to be merely innocent!

With a rug, shawl and gloves provided by a Russian friend, Dukes was able to sleep more soundly in the tomb and spent four nights there, claiming even to have some affection for it.

Peter Petrovich had now left for Finland by means of Agar's secret night-time rendezvous and, in the meantime, Dukes had managed to obtain some further papers belonging to a draughtsman who worked in a factory on the outskirts of the city. Alexander Bankau, as Dukes was now known, duly took up lodgings in the room which Peter had continued to let. Bankau, whatever his other merits, did not have exemption from military service and Dukes, aware that he must try to remain in touch with events at the centre, enlisted into the automobile section of the 8th Army in late May 1919. An attachment to this section afforded him greater freedom of movement and advantage over civilians when obtaining accommodation, leisure or travel and also ensured better rations. Fortunately, his commander was a White sympathiser who had been obliged to join the Red forces. This provided Dukes with some additional latitude and enabled him to observe closely the response of the population, Bolshevik or not, to the mutiny of Krasnaya Gorka and its aftermath. The repressive measures that ensued placed even greater strain on Dukes and his network of agents.

Dukes's position was also aggravated by a severe shortage of cash. Money infiltrated by Petrovich from Agar and British Intelligence on investigation turned out to be counterfeit and of poor quality. Yet money was vital for his work besides his own survival. His agents, whether working to him directly or through third parties had all to be paid in cash or kind. His agents in Moscow expected a fixed salary and others required food and money. Money was essential for lodging, food, clothing, travel, sending couriers, paying 'sack-men' and agents, purchasing information, tipping, bribing, and all kinds of emergencies. Eventually Dukes decided to reacquaint himself with one of the few Englishmen still living in the city and ask him for money. This man, whom Dukes referred to as 'Mr George', probably the George E. Gibson who subsequently made a claim on the Treasury for repayment of this money, had originally represented the British Shipping Company in Petrograd. Like several other British people remaining in Russia, he was a leading figure in the various British committees and relief bodies which then existed, and was in contact with the British Home Office by means of Dukes and the courier service operated by him. It was this connection, when identified by the *Cheka*, that led to Gibson's subsequent arrest and imprisonment. In fact, Gibson helped Dukes on several occasions. Dukes was previously introduced to Gibson as Paul Pavlovitch, and gave him a receipt signed 'Captain Philip McNeill', a name which would be recognised by his intelligence masters in Finland, Latvia or Estonia. And, although Dukes did not divulge this in his memoirs, he convinced Gibson that the latter should also help his (Dukes's) replacement in the event of his demise.

Whatever the shortcomings of Peter Petrovich's quarters - a 'dusty, mouldy and vermin-ridden cell' - Dukes at least found safety there and peace in which to compile his reports. It also served as a base for visits to his agents and to political meetings:

As 'Comrade Bankau', Communist, on active Red Army duty, but delegated to Petrograd by a friendly commander . . . for various missions which it was nobody's business but his to enquire into, my days succeeded each other with a relatively tranquil flow which was peace itself compared with what had gone before. I was readily accepted into the local Party circle, where genuine musical abilities added lustre to the hall of a fictitious record of past martyrdom, while carefully simulated weak health relieved me of special duties.

Dukes discovered that his party ticket was an 'open sesame', providing, among other things, free travel. On the one hand, his proximity to many Communist Party members demanded absolute vigilance. On the other, he had great latitude to read, write and make notes. Of the daring episodes of this period, Dukes mentioned the moment at which he managed to fulfil a personal ambition by attending meetings of the Petrograd Soviet as the official guest for his regiment. This distinction allowed him to sit and vote in the plenary meetings of the Soviet and, from the point of view of intelligence gathering, monitor the atmosphere of the place, the nature of the discussions taking place and the movements of Zinoviev and Evdokimov and other senior party figures. Such activities were fraught with risks as *Cheka* agents invariably infiltrated meetings and one unguarded movement would have alerted them to his presence. As the packed hall would listen in silence, Zinoviev would threaten with death those spies of the Allies that he knew to be among the audience.

Yet Dukes, like his masters in London, realised that he was living on borrowed time and he decided that if Petrovich, his courier, did not arrive on the second of the two appointed dates (he had already told him he would not make the first) he would swim the necessary two miles into the icy waters of the Gulf of Finland to meet Agar in the torpedo boat. With typical resolve Dukes began to train for this, smearing himself with grease and lying for long periods in cold baths. On the first night Petrovich arrived but he had been spotted by a patrol. As Dukes had at the last moment decided to delay his departure in order to complete vital work, Petrovich started out on his return trip through Estonia to warn Agar that he must use a different route on his next trip as the *Cheka* would now regularly patrol the seashore. However, he did not get back in time to stop Agar and, as expected, searchlights at Kronstadt detected the torpedo boat. On the occasion of the final rendezvous, a different courier, Gefter, appeared. After some problems, he managed to secure a vessel to replace the skiff that he had lost. After many emotional farewells, Dukes and Gefter rowed into the dark and cold waters but found it increasingly difficult to steer their boat. The weather changed and, to their horror, they discovered that the boat had a fish well and was filling with water. Forced to head for shore, the boat sank and they swam the remaining half-mile to the shore. Gefter had thrown his boots away and this, combined with fatigue, a close encounter with a foot patrol, and hunger as they walked back towards Petrograd, led Gefter to collapse and to stop breathing; Dukes, with typical initiative, managed to save him by means of artificial respiration.

After a final visit to Moscow, Dukes had one last chance to meet up with Agar. However, the Bolsheviks had taken measures to strengthen their coastal defences and patrols and it became impossible to venture anywhere near the shores of the Gulf. Agar had in fact encountered problems himself. Having been caught by searchlights at Kronstadt, he crashed onto one of the Kronstadt forts and then drifted towards the Finnish coast where his boat was towed into shallow waters by Finnish craft. Happily for Dukes, however, Peter Petrovich turned up again. With a fellow-conspirator whose family had taken refuge in Latvia, Dukes and Petrovich, equipped with small bags of salt (each of them containing Dukes's secret reports), piled onto a train full of foraging Russians and headed out of Petrograd:

> There sandwiched, I had all night in which to ponder upon the strange existence I had so long led and which was now drawing to a close. The figures of 'McNeill', 'Ilitch', 'Afirenko', 'Krylenko', 'Markovitch', 'Bankau' passed in intimate, yet already receding, review, with the clear-cut images of Melnikov, Murometz,

Stepanovna, Zorinsky; the Doctor, Policeman . . . the gallant 'Mr. George'. . . . Weird, fascinating, ghostly and yet intensely real panorama: panorama too, of hopes and fears, laughter and tears, guile, stratagem and intrigue, great terrors, and greater loves.

Having narrowly escaped detection when the train was stopped and searched in the middle of the night, the party crossed Lake Luban, which marked the Russian–Latvian frontier, and was there dragged off to a local Latvian Commandant. He, almost pathologically angry, insisted that they were Red spies and almost had them shot, the secret reports that had been clearly addressed alone saving them.

* * *

If Dukes had any clear ideas of what he might do on his return to England, he certainly could not have predicted the course taken by the remaining years of his life. In London, after a meeting with members of the Cabinet, he quickly found that he was at the centre of a political and media storm and, rather like Ronald Sinclair, accused by the Bolsheviks of all manner of things. In Dukes's case the charges centred on his alleged conspiratorial activities whilst in Russia. Dukes defended himself vigorously but his identity as Britain's top agent in Russia was soon common knowledge. As such, further employment by SIS was practically ruled out, assuming, of course, Dukes would have desired it. Instead, it seems that, for a time immediately after his return, he turned to journalism, writing a series of articles in *The Times*, in which he recounted episodes from his period in Russia. Yet not all of what he wrote was well received. In September 1919, he was drawn into a public dispute, albeit a good-natured one, in the columns of the *Daily Chronicle* with his brother Ashley Dukes, the author and dramatist. This centred on how Britain should respond to the situation in Russia and Dukes, who was to a point sympathetic to the principles of the revolution and who advocated a humanitarian approach on the part of the British, was strongly criticised and labelled a 'spy' and 'agent'. At the time of his return, senior Foreign Office officials had discussed the possibility that Dukes might compromise himself and the interventionist cause by rushing into print. And there was certainly much in what Dukes told that might lend weight to that cause. When he left Petrograd the city was on the verge of starvation. His newspaper articles revealed that, in his view, the mass of the Russian population was opposed to communism. Quite simply, if Britain did not intervene then Germany would and, according to Dukes, their influence was steadily growing in the adjoining countries of the Baltic.

There was also concern that the Soviet government might misconstrue his proposed knighthood as a reward for his supposed conspiratorial activities. Precisely at that time, the British and Soviet governments were involved in delicate negotiations to arrange a swap of prisoners and Dukes's former colleagues in SIS were also involved in this operation. By September 1920, Dukes was in Poland, reporting on the developing conflict between Russia and Poland. There, writing to a friend, he noted the omnivorous local vermin and requested the despatch of some tins of 'Keating's' powder, to keep them at bay. Again, the Foreign Office was concerned at Dukes activities, forwarding instructions that no help should be given to him to reach the front. Had he done so it was feared that the Bolshevik regime would find out and would interpret this as British support for the Polish offensive. In fact, that was precisely what Dukes hoped for. In an article in *The Times* in January 1921, he claimed that if Britain allowed Poland to succumb to the Soviet advance, it would mean 'chaos in Europe'.

As previously noted, Dukes also became involved in official discussions about compensating the British community in Russia. In particular, several claims had been made on behalf of individuals who claimed either to have helped Dukes in his work or to have suffered as a result of his activities. George Gibson, who had on several occasions provided Dukes with funds and other support, had repeatedly presented his claims to the Foreign Office but without success. Dukes, by then on a lecture tour in America, wrote privately to a friend at the Foreign Office that Gibson planned to raise the matter in the press and that he, Dukes, would support him. He proposed to do so by renouncing his knighthood and by publicising it in his book. As he pointed out, he had been obliged to seek Gibson's help because the counterfeit money provided by the British Government had been unusable.

If nothing else, such activities must surely have precluded further employment of Dukes by SIS. As we have seen, the postwar world of retrenchment was not congenial for ageing spies. Dukes's later business interests, his extensive lecture tours overseas and his propaganda work undertaken in the Second World War, might suggest that he could still be of use to his former masters, but it seems that for one reason or another he was not used. Robin Bruce Lockhart in his book, Reilly, Ace of Spies, suggests that Dukes was, in fact, almost turned down by Mansfield Cumming for his posting in Russia and was taken on largely because of his expression of interest in Cumming's collection of pistols. Yet his success as an agent was remarkable and, but for his slightly wayward and headstrong nature at times, he might have risen far in the Secret Service. As it was, besides his business interests and lecturing, he continued to write and to capitalise on his Russian experiences and, towards the end of his life, became something of a yoga guru.

* * *

Although decades have passed since Dukes and these intrepid intelligence gatherers and analysts ceased their activities, their concerns remain highly relevant. In the case of the Soviet Union, with the passing of Zirinovsky, the overblown nationalist, the spectre of a resurgent Russia appears to have receded. Yet it is open to question quite how long Putin will be content to play second fiddle to President Bush. Also, it is not so very long since Russian tanks again rolled through the Caucasus on what, in the last millennium or so, has for the Russian soldier become a familiar perambulation. And, whilst in the present turbulent state of world affairs we do not perceive malevolent and ubiquitous Russian influence, those troublespots still exist. Whether in Soane's Kurdistan or Persia, or the Ottoman Turkey and Mesopotamia of his day and that of William Childs, issues of nationality, irredentism, borders and now, of course, oil and soon, water, continue to bedevil international affairs and therefore to place a continued demand on Britain's eyes and ears in those regions – her intelligence agents.

Similarly, just as Ronald Sinclair turned his attention to Kashmir in the 1940s, that issue has again come to the fore and, regrettably, in a context that bears marked similarities to the world after 1918. Since the Soviet–Afghan War, investigative reporters have uncovered many terrorist cells which, if they do not form a network as such, have yet possessed sufficient common ground to engineer atrocities. And, just as they did in the 1920s, officials have now inexorably come to see behind these terrible acts, a single evil genius, a dark lord almost; it's a theme that continues to haunt the official psyche. The evil genius has, of course, now been traced to Osama bin Laden and his alleged extensive contacts that span all Muslim countries of the earth and encompass also, pockets or cells of extreme Muslim sentiment in the West. The parallels with Norman Bray's investigations are marked. The scope of the trouble, the terrorist training schools, the same confusions between intelligence bodies, between paranoia and vested interests, and the same inability to understand the source of these troubles, all characterise official responses now as then. And, of course, the fear in the 1920s, that events in Nigeria, or Egypt or Iraq might flare into a broader conflagration apply now with even greater force.

The differences, such as they exist, simply seem to emphasise the value of the spy. The stakes are now higher, with weapons of mass destruction drawn into the equation. Vast sums of money are spent and technology is harnessed on both sides in this new battle of wits and, unlike the 1920s, genuine international cooperation in rooting out terrorist elements has emerged. Yet on one level at least, the point is inescapable: as long as such threats exist, the spy in whatever guise will remain indispensable.

Further Intelligence

Bibliography

UNPUBLISHED SOURCES

Public Record Office, London

Admiralty Papers

ADM 1:	Navy Department: Correspondence and Papers
ADM 12:	Digests and Indexes
ADM 116:	Case Files
ADM 137:	Historical Section: Records used for Official History, First World War
ADM 177:	*Navy Lists*, Confidential Edition
ADM 186:	Publications
ADM 196:	Officers' Service Records (Series III)

Air Ministry Records

AIR 8:	Department of the Chief of the Air Staff: Registered Files
AIR 19:	Air Department: Private Office Papers
AIR 30:	Submission Papers to Sovereign
AIR 76:	Department of the Master-General of Personnel: Officers' Service Records

Records of the Board of Trade

BT 11:	Commercial Relations and Exports Department and Predecessors

Registered Files and Other Records

BT 13:	Establishment Department: Correspondence and Papers
BT 60:	Department of Overseas Trade: Correspondence and Papers
BT 61:	Department of Overseas Trade: Establishment Files
BT 196:	Confidential Reports on Activities

Bibliography

Cabinet Office Records

CAB 1:   Miscellaneous Records

CAB 4:   Committee of Imperial Defence (CID): Miscellaneous Memoranda (B Series)

CAB 6:   CID: Defence of India Memoranda (D Series)

CAB 16:   CID, Ad Hoc Sub-Committees: Minutes, Memoranda and Reports

CAB 17:   CID: Miscellaneous Correspondence and Memoranda

CAB 21:   Cabinet Office and Predecessors: Registered Files

CAB 23:   Minutes

CAB 24:   Memoranda (GT, CP and G War Series)

CAB 27:   Miscellaneous Committees: Records (General Series)

CAB 44:   CID, Historical Branch and Cabinet Office, Historical Section: War Histories: Draft Chapters and Narratives, Military

CAB 45:   CID, Historical Branch and Cabinet Office, Historical Section: Official War Histories Correspondence and Papers

CAB 103:   Historical Section: Registered Files (HS and Other Series)

Records of the Central Criminal Court

CRIM 1:   Central Criminal Court: Depositions

Colonial Office Records

CO 323:   Colonies, General: Original Correspondence

CO 583:   Nigeria Original Correspondence

CO 730:   Iraq Original Correspondence

CO 732:   Middle East Original Correspondence

CO 781:   Iraq Register of Correspondence

CO 850:   Personnel: Original Correspondence

CO 852:   Economic General Department and Predecessors: Registered Files

CO 968:   Defence Department and Successors: Original Correspondence

Foreign Office Records

FO 78:   Political and Other Departments: General Correspondence before 1906, Ottoman Empire

FO 195:   Embassy and Consulates, Turkey (formerly Ottoman Empire): General Correspondence

FO 197:   Embassy and Consulates, Turkey (formerly Ottoman Empire): Registers of Correspondence

FO 368:   Commercial and Sanitary Department: General Correspondence from 1906

FO 369:   Consular Department: General Correspondence from 1906

FO 370:   Library and the Research Department: General Correspondence from 1906

FO 373:   Peace Conference of 1919 to 1920: Handbooks

FO 566:   Registers of General Correspondence

FO 608:   Peace Conference: British Delegation, Correspondence and Papers

FO 610:   Chief Clerk's Department and Passport Office: Passport Registers

FO 611:   Chief Clerk's Department and Passport Office: Passport Registers' Indexes of Names

FO 686:   Jedda Agency: Papers

FO 800:   Private Offices: Various Ministers' and Officials' Papers

FO 882:   Arab Bureau: Correspondence and Reports

FO 1011:   Loraine Papers

Records of the Secret Service
HD 3:   Foreign Office: Permanent Under-Secretary's Department: Correspondence and Papers

Records of the Security Service
KV 1:   First World War Historical Reports and Other Papers

KV 3:   Subject (SF Series) Files

KV 4:   Policy (Pol F Series) Files

Records of the Paymaster General
PMG 4:   Army Establishment: Half Pay

Treasury Records
T 1:   Papers

T 2:   Registers of Papers

T 108:   Subject Registers

T 165:   Blue Notes

War Office Papers
WO 32:   Registered Files (General Series)

WO 33:   Reports, Memoranda and Papers (O and A Series)

WO 106:   Directorate of Military Operations and Military Intelligence, and Predecessors: Correspondence and Papers

WO 208:   Directorate of Military Operations and Intelligence, and Directorate of Military Intelligence; Ministry of Defence, Defence Intelligence Staff: Files

WO 216:   Office of the Chief of the Imperial General Staff: Papers

WO 339:   Officers' Services, First World War, Long Number Papers (Numerical)

WO 374:   Officers' Services, First World War, Personal Files (Alphabetical)

Records of the Prime Minister's Office
PREM 3:   Operational Correspondence and Papers

Records of the Ministry of Defence
DEFE 1:   Postal and Telegraph Censorship Department, Predecessors and Successor: Papers

Records of the Ministry of Information
INF 4:   War of 1914 to 1918 Information Services

Records of the Special Operations Executive
HS 7:   Histories and War Diaries: Registered Files

Gifts and Deposits
PRO 30/40:   Papers of Sir John Ardagh

Rhodes House Library, Oxford

Papers of G.J. Lethem

National Library of Scotland

Blackwood Papers

National Library of Ireland

O'Malley Papers

Northamptonshire Record Office

Diaries of Lord Exeter

Bibliography

Imperial War Museum, London

Diaries of Sir Walter Kirke
Papers of Ronald Sinclair
Papers of C.B. Stokes
Papers and Diaries of Sir V. Kell

Liddell Hart Centre for Military Archives, King's College, London

Liddell Hart Papers
Papers of Sir James Edmonds

British Library, London

Letters from T.E. Shaw (Lawrence) to C.F. Shaw
Papers of Arnold Talbot Wilson

Oriental and India Office Collections

L/P+J/6 Series
L/P+J/12 Series
L/P+S/10 Series
L/P+S/11 Series
L/P+S/18 Series
L/MIL/9 Series
L/MIL/17 Series

European Manuscript Collections

Montagu Papers
Diaries of S.F. Muspratt
Curzon Papers
Bailey Papers
Lorimer Papers
Sinclair Papers

Cambridge University Library

Hardinge Papers
Templewood Papers
Baldwin Papers

Nuffield College, Oxford

Mottistone Papers

Churchill Archives Centre, Cambridge

O'Conor Papers
Hyde Papers
Chartwell Papers
Headlam-Morley Papers
Lloyd Papers

Middle East Centre, Oxford

R.M. Graves Papers
Deedes Papers
Hay Papers
Hamilton Papers
Davies Papers
Edmonds Papers
Whittall & Co.

British Library of Political and Economic Science

C.K. Webster Papers

Royal Institute of International Affairs

Papers Relating to the Paris Peace Conference

Royal Geographical Society

Papers of H. Vischer
Papers of F.R. Rodd

THESES

Fraser, T.G., 'The Intrigues of the German Government and the Gahdr Party Against British Rule in India, 1914–1918', University of London, PhD, 1974

Bibliography

Occleshaw, M.E., 'British Military Intelligence in the First World War', University of Keele, PhD, 1984

Powe, M.B., 'The Emergence of the War Department Intelligence Agency: 1885–1918', University of Kansas, MA, 1974

PUBLISHED SOURCES

Newspapers

The Times
The *Daily Chronicle*
The *Morning Post*
The *Army, Navy and Air Force Gazette*
Army Quarterly
The *Forum*
Cornhill Magazine
Blackwoods Magazine
Asian Review
The *Spectator*
The *Christian Commonwealth*
Kelly's Directory

Official Publications

London Gazette
Army List
Navy List
Air Force List
War Office List
Foreign Office List
Hansard
Colonial Office List

BOOKS AND ARTICLES

Unless otherwise stated, all titles published in London.

Adelson, R., *Portrait of an Amateur* (1975)
Agar, A., *Baltic Episode* (1963)

Allason, R., *The Branch* (1983)

Andrew, C.M., *Secret Service: The Making of the British Intelligence Community* (1985)

——, 'The British Secret Service and Anglo-Soviet Relations in the 1920s. Part 1', *Historical Journal*, vol. 20, 1977

Aston, Sir George, *Secret Service* (1930)

Baden-Powell, Lt-Gen., Sir, *My Adventures as a Spy* (1915)

Bailey, F.M., *Mission to Tashkent*, with introduction by P. Hopkirk (Oxford, 1992)

Beesly, P., *Room 40. British Naval Intelligence, 1914–1918* (Oxford, 1984)

——, 'British Intelligence in Two World Wars, Some Similarities and Differences', in *Intelligence and International Relations, 1900 to 1945*, eds C. Andrew and J. Noakes (Exeter, 1987)

Boucard, R., *Revelations from the Secret Service* (1930)

Boyle, A., *The Riddle of Erskine Childers* (1977)

Bray, N.N.E., *Shifting Sands* (1934)

Brook-Shepherd, G., *The Storm Petrels* (1977)

——, *Iron Maze: The Western Secret Services and the Bolsheviks* (1998)

Buchan, J., *The Thirty-Nine Steps* (1915)

——, *Greenmantle* (1916)

——, *Mr Standfast* (1919)

——, *The Three Hostages* (1924)

——, *The Island of Sheep* (1936)

Bullard, Sir R., *The Camels Must Go, an Autobiography* (1961)

Burnaby, F., *On Horseback Through Asia Minor*, with introduction by P. Hopkirk (Oxford, 1996)

——, *A Ride to Khiva*, with introduction by P. Hopkirk (Oxford, 1997)

Capelotti, P.J., *Our Man in the Crimea: Commander Hugo Koehler and the Russian Civil War* (Columbia, USA, 1991)

Charmley, J., *Lord Lloyd and the Decline of the British Empire* (1987)

Childers, E., *The Riddle of the Sands* (1903)

Childs, W.J., *Across Asia Minor on Foot* (Edinburgh, 1917)
(see also Childs's articles mainly in *Blackwoods Magazine* between July 1915 and August 1916)

Chirol, V., *Indian Unrest* (1910)

Cobban, A., *Ambassadors and Secret Agents* (1954)

Cole, J.A., *Prince of Spies: Henri Le Caron* (1984)

Cox, M. ed., *The Oxford Book of Spy Stories* (Oxford etc., 1997)

Deacon, R., *A History of the British Secret Service* (1969)

Dilks, D.N., 'Flashes of Intelligence: The Foreign Office, the SIS and Security before the Second World War', in Andrew, C.M., and Dilks, D.N., *The Missing Dimension: Governments and Intelligence Communities in the Twentieth Century* (1984)

Dukes, Sir Paul, *Red Dusk and the Morrow* (1922)

——, *The Story of "ST25": Adventure and Romance in the Secret Intelligence Service in Red Russia* (1938)

Edmonds, C.J., *Kurds, Turks and Arabs* (Toronto/New York, 1957)

Ellis, C.H., *Transcaspian Episode* (1963)

Felstead, S.T., *German Spies at Bay* (1920)

——, ed., *Steinhaur: The Kaiser's Master Spy. The Story as Told by Himself* (1930)

Fisher, J.N., 'The Interdepartmental Committee on Eastern Unrest and British responses to Bolshevik and other intrigues against her empire during the 1920s', *Journal of Asian History* (2000)

Fitch, H.T., *Traitors Within* (1933)

Fitzherbert, M., *The Man Who Was Greenmantle* (1983)

French, D., 'Spy Fever in Britain', *Historical Journal*, vol. 21, 1978

Gandy, C., 'Fez and Frock-Coat: A Very English Consul in Ottoman Turkey', *Journal of the Royal Society for Asian Affairs*, 1984

Gaunt, Sir G., *The Yield of Years: A Story of Adventure Afloat and Ashore* (1940)

Gokay, B., *A Clash of Empires: Turkey Between Russian Bolshevism and British Imperialism, 1918–1923* (1997)

Goldstein, E., 'Historians Outside the Academy: G.W. Prothero and the Experience of the Foreign Office Historical Section, 1917–20', *Bulletin of the Institute of Historical Research* (1990)

——, 'Hertford House: The Naval Intelligence Geographical Section and Peace Conference Planning, 1917–1919', *Mariner's Mirror* (1986)

Griffiths, Sir P., *'To Guard my People': The History of the Indian Police* (1971)

Hamilton, K.A., 'The Pursuit of Enlightened Patriotism: The British Foreign Office and Historical Researchers during the Great War and its Aftermath', *Bulletin of the Institute of Historical Research* (1988)

Hanioglu, M.S., 'Notes on the Young Turks and the Freemasons, 1875–1908', *Middle Eastern Studies* (1989)

Hiley, N.P., 'The Failure of British Espionage Against Germany, 1907–1914', *Historical Journal*, vol. 26, 1983

Hill, G.A., *Go Spy the Land* (1932)

Hoare, Sir S., *The Fourth Seal* (1930)

Bibliography

Hohler, T.B., *Diplomatic Petrel* (1942)

Hopkirk, P., *Setting the East Ablaze. Lenin's Dream of an Empire in Asia* (Oxford, 1986)

——, *The Great Game. On Secret Service in High Asia* (1990)

——, *On Secret Service East of Constantinople* (1994)

Huntford, R., *Shackleton* (1985)

Hyde, H. Montgomery, *British Security Coordination: The Secret History of British Intelligence in the Americas, 1940–45*, introduction by N. West (1998)

——, *The Quiet Canadian* (1962)

——, *Secret Intelligence Agent* (1982)

Ibrahim, H.A., 'The Development of Economic and Political Neo-Mahdism in the Sudan 1926–1935', *Sudan Notes and Records* (1977)

——, 'Imperialism and Neo-Mahdism in the Sudan: A study of British Policy Towards Neo-Mahdism, 1924–1927', *International Journal of African Historical Studies* (1980)

Judd, A., *The Quest for Mansfield Cumming and the Founding of the Secret Service* (1999)

Keay, J., *Eccentric Travellers* (1982)

Kedourie, E., 'Young Turks, Freemasons and Jews', *Middle Eastern Studies* (1971)

Kettle, M., *Sidney Reilly: The True Story* (1983)

Kipling, R., *Kim* (1901)

Kirkwood, D., *My Life of Revolt* (1935)

Knightly, P., *The First Casualty: The War Correspondent as Hero and Myth-Maker from the Crimea to Kosovo*, 2nd edn (2000)

Landau, H., *Secrets of the White Lady* (New York, 1935)

——, *Spreading the Spy Net* (1938)

Lawson, J.C., *Tales of Aegean Intrigue* (1920)

Le Queux, W., *England's Peril: A Story of the Secret Service* (1900)

——, *Secrets of the Foreign Office* (1903)

——, *Things I Know* (1923)

——, *The Invasion of 1910* (1906)

——, *Spies of the Kaiser: Plotting the Downfall of England* (1909)

——, *German Spies in England* (1915)

Linklater, A., *Compton Mackenzie, A Life* (1992)

Lockhart, R.B., *Memoirs of a British Agent* (1934)

——, *Reilly, Ace of Spies* (1967)

Macartney, W., *Zig-Zag* (1938)

Macfie, A.L., 'British Intelligence and the Causes of Unrest in Mesopotamia, 1919–21, *Middle Eastern Studies* (1999)

Bibliography

Mackenzie, C., *Gallipoli Memories* (1929)
——, *Athenian Memories* (1931)
——, *Greek Memories* (1932)
——, *Aegean Memories* (1940)
Meynell, F., *My Lives* (1971)
Morris, L.P., 'British Secret Service History in Khorassan, 1887–1908', *Historical Journal*, vol. 27, 1984
Neilson, K. '"Joy Rides"?: British Intelligence and Propaganda in Russia 1914–1917', *Historical Journal*, vol. 24, 1981
Nichols, B., *25* (1926)
Pares, Sir E., *40 Years in Constantinople, 1873 to 1915* (1916)
Paris, T.J., 'British Middle East Policy Making After the First World War: The Lawrentian and Wilsonian Schools', *Historical Journal* (1998)
Philby, K., *My Silent War* (1968)
Platt, D.C.M., *The Cinderella Service: British Consuls Since 1825* (1971)
Popplewell, R.J., *Intelligence and the Defence of the Indian Empire, 1904–1924* (1995)
——, 'The Surveillance of Indian "Seditionists" in North America, 1905–1915', in eds Andrew, C.M. and Noakes, J., *Intelligence and International Relations 1900–1945* (Exeter, 1987)
——, 'The Surveillance of Indian Revolutionaries in Great Britain and on the Continent, 1903–1914', *Intelligence and National Security*, vol. 3, 1988
Porter, B., *The Origins of the Vigilante State. The London Metropolitan Police Special Branch before the First World War* (1987)
——, *Plots and Paranoia. A History of Political Espionage in Britain, 1790–1988* (1989)
Read, A., and Fisher, D., *Colonel Z. The Secret Life of a Master of Spies* (1984)
Sheffy, Y., *British Military Intelligence in the Palestine Campaign, 1914–18* (1998)
Sinclair, R., *The Spy Who Disappeared: Diary of a Secret Mission to Russian Central Asia in 1918*, introduction and epilogue by Peter Hopkirk (1990)
——, *Adventures in Persia* (1988)
Taylor, P.M., *Confessions of a Thug* (Oxford, 1986)
Thomson, B., *Queer People* (1922)
——, *The Scene Changes* (1939)
——, *The Allied Secret Service in Greece* (1931)
Thwaites, N., *Velvet and Vinegar* (1932)

Tibenderana, P.K., 'The Role of the British Administration in the Appointment of the Emirs of Northern Nigeria, 1903–1931: The Case of Sokoto Province', *Journal of African History* (1987)

Townshend, A.F., *A Military Consul in Turkey* (1910)

Ubah, C.N., 'Problems of Christian Missionaries in the Muslim Emirates of Nigeria, 1900–1928', *Journal of African Studies* (1976)

——, 'British Measures Against Mahdism at Dumbulwa in Northern Nigeria, 1923: A Case of Colonial Overreaction', *Islamic Culture* (1976)

Vischer, H., *Across the Sahara* (1910)

Warburg, G., 'British Policy Towards the Ansar in Sudan: A Note on Historical Controversy', *Middle Eastern Studies* (1997)

West, N., *MI6: British Secret Intelligence Service Operations 1909–1945* (1983)

Winstone, H.V.F., *The Illicit Adventure: The Story of Political and Military Intelligence in the Middle East from 1898 to 1926* (1982)

Yilmaz, S., 'An Ottoman Warrior Abroad: Enver Pasa as an Expatriate', *Middle Eastern Studies* (1999)

Young, R.J., ed., *The Diaries of Sir Robert Bruce Lockhart, vol. 1: 1915–1938* (1973)

Index

Places

Index

Index

General